Reflections from the Silence

Copyright © 2021 Robert H. Wellington

This book is a work of fiction. People, places, events, and situations are the products of the authors imagination. Any resemblance to persons, living or dead, or historical events, are purely coincidental.

All rights reserved. No part of this book may be reproduced, distributed, or transmitted in any form or by any means, including photocopying, recording, or other electronic or mechanical methods, without prior written permission from the publisher or author, except in the case of brief quotations embodied in critical reviews and certain other noncommercial uses permitted by copyright law.

Library of Congress Control Number	2021922541
Paperback	978-1-68547-024-1
Hardcover	978-1-68547-025-8
eBook	978-1-68547-026-5

Published 05/11/2021
Printed in the United States of America

FRISCO, TX 75034
United States

www.wa-publishing.com

Reflections *from the* SILENCE

Robert H. Wellington

Foreword

These writings found their way to my journals during four decades of meditation and journaling. They are universal in nature. They found their way from the Silence, through me and out my pen. They are from the quiet realms and are available to all who search. Although they came through me, they are not mine alone. They are ours. As you read them, close your eyes, slow your breathing and quiet your mind. I think you will find you too carry these ideas, and so many more, deep inside.

I have included herein, 365 thoughts, inspirations, poems and essays. Feel free to read them all at once, one each day or however the Spirit moves you. Perhaps you will use them as seed thoughts in meditation, or as daily companions to address the challenges of each new day. They are meant to be gifts to the open hearts led to these pages. They are reflections from the silence. Their beauty lies deep within. Think about them. Contemplate their meaning. These ideas and mini-revelations have guided me as a husband, father, grandfather, brother, small business owner and friend. Yet, I have barely plumbed their depth. I invite you to go deep inside and discover their full beauty, discover the majesty of the silence. Here you will discover more than ideas and concepts; here you will discover yourself.

Introduction

The Silence, what is it? Where does it reside? What secrets does it hold? What is its magic? Some think of the Silence as a void or vacuum; Some as a physical place where the chaos of the world has been set aside and only the faint presence of creative potential resides. Some do not believe that it exists at all. For those who have been touched by the secrets of the silence, an overwhelming need to find it begins to direct their path. Each who searches finds himself or herself on a unique quest, for in Silence is all potential, waiting only for the vibratory thought of creation to direct each journey. The Silence is never far. It is within each of us. We have only to listen for it, by first quieting the senses and then the mind. When we hear nothing, we have found it, the home of truth and all possibilities. Bask in its peaceful presence. Soon you will begin to resonate with it. At that moment its secrets are revealed. Returning from the meditative mountain, we bring the reflection of these truths, back to the physical plane. We try to express these reflections through artistic expression or poetry but fall short of releasing their true essence. The densities in the 3d world cannot vibrate at a level high enough to fully free their beauty, and only the reflections remain. But all is not lost. The secrets of the reflections cannot find a home in the intellect, but they are fully recognized, as kin, by the heart. Listen to the Heart and it will lead you back to the Silence. With each visit, we bring back more of the wonder of the Silence, and slowly raise the frequency of our earthly home, until heaven and earth begin to , again, vibrate as one. This is the Spiritual Quest, holy evolution, the journey to the One, the journey Home.

Blessings to all who embark on this journey, my fellow travelers, companions and co-workers. Together, **We will Heal this World, One Encounter at a Time**. Together we participate in the greatest of all adventures, the journey home.

As a general note and matter of convenience, I sometimes use he to the exclusion of she. Please interpret he as he/she, for you cannot have one without the other.

And So It Begins...

1

The beingness of a humble, striving and loving man is the essence of a Holy One.

2

By giving we receive. Through giving, eternal treasures are stored in heaven. We cannot truly give without receiving. We cannot receive without giving

3

We enter through the gate by becoming the gate. We spread Love throughout the world by becoming Love.

4

Search for the wisdom to be unattached and you will find yourself in the middle observing the pairs of opposites, while totally unaffected by them. You have found peace, while all around you is chaos.

5

The glorious essence, which is us, need only be glimpsed for a moment and the door to eternity is revealed.

6

Sense Love and sense the Soul. Know Love and reunite with the Soul.

7

True sacrifice is any thought or act which puts God ahead of the lower self.

8

It is important to remember that the God/Love in ourselves is the same God/Love in our neighbors and all that exists. We must first find God in ourselves, before we can truly know it in others

9

A true sage makes himself a way and not an end.

10

That which is hidden from mortal mind longs to be seen.

11

One cannot truly root oneself in heaven, if any roots remain attached to the earth.

12

Expansion of consciousness and the actualization of that expansion through right action and sacrificial loving service is the Path.

13

Light in some ways is Love consciously recognized and expressed as wisdom.

14

By sensing all that is around us on the physical plane, we sometimes see ourselves as separate and distinct. This is the great stumbling block. We must see ourselves and all that exists as intimately connected, a part of the unified whole.

15

See yourself in the light as the light. See yourself in everything and everything in yourself. For you are one with the creator of all things. Remember.

Leadership

16

Leadership is the process of becoming the path for others to sense and to follow. The leader is the light which others sense and are drawn to. True leadership is service on a higher turn of the wheel.

17

Leadership appeals to the followers true self like a magnet to iron. The leader leads with his/her light, but is also guided by a greater light. And so it goes, an endless chain of light, on the endless path back to the Father.

18

The leader is the expression of Love. The leader is the embodiment of compassion. The leader's senses are controlled, for he knows he is greater than the senses. He is wisdom.

19

The leader uses form to serve, but knows he is not the form.

20

Let Love be your guide, love-wisdom be your essence and service to the greater, your purpose.

21

The leader is not necessarily motivated by results, but rather, the inner growth of those he/she leads.

22

Leadership grows within the individual in direct proportion to one's recognition of the divinity within

23

The Path

Long ago they made a choice,

To sing His song, to follow His voice.

Though seemingly quite all alone,

Yet many walk the pathway home.

They walk the path of subtle truth.

They search for light, they long for proof.

So many times they trip and fall.

Though ridiculed, they still stand tall.

They pick themselves, up off the ground,

And thank the sky for wisdom found.

For every misstep when corrected,

Reveals a gem so long neglected.

A gem which holds within its light,

The secrets that give wings for flight.

Their Magic resting in the deep,

Awaiting to be raised from sleep.

So many steps and lessons learned.

Their chests explode with hearts that yearn,

To guide them, to more light to share,

A gift so fine, a prize so rare.

They turn within and search so deep.

The answers there, to share not keep.

And through this sharing, more is gathered,

The seeds soon grow, from many scattered.

And others wake to join the quest,

To share the truth, to wake the rest.

No longer separate, now they're One.

Pure loving essence, they've become,

The very answers that they seek.

The truth of which the heavens speak.

24

Silence is the natural result of sensing His song and letting it resonate through you and out into the world, healing without making a sound.

25

Purification

Purification is the process of becoming universal. It is the journey from separation to oneness. Negativism, criticism, anger, greed, jealousy and hatred are polluting thoughts and acts. They are states of mind precipitated by the belief that we are separate from all that exists. These thoughts cannot exist within the universal mind. For if we are a part of the whole, who or what is there to hate, to feel jealous towards, or to criticize.

26

The one who selflessly gives all to others, receives the bounty of the cosmos.

27

To know the higher, strive to vibrate in resonance with the higher. When one is full of Love and givingness, that one soon sees with an open eye all which moves the universe.

28

Life provides the gauntlet through which each must run. Through effort comes growth.

29

Focused Striving

Spiritually focused striving, slowly results in a clear and controlled mind while reflecting the growing recognition of the love within. It is a light or energy which permeates every aspect of our being, influencing our thoughts, actions and words. We, at first, see this light as an influencing aspect of our being. In time, however, it becomes ever more apparent that we are the light. We are the love, and all the other personality pretenders to our outward expression merely imperfect reflections of our true being, like distorted reflections on a stormy lake. This recognition of his or her true being continues to grow as she or he learns to recognize and embrace the vibrations of being.

30

See that which you love in all that you encounter and you will soon come face to face with your true self.

31

Our eyes see by the reflection of light off the form. Our heart sees by the reflection of love off the Self.

32

Controlling the Senses

The control of the senses through the mind is a practice of vigilance with respect to our desires. Controlling the senses is a process of purification, discernment, selfless service and the quieting of the mind through meditation and prayer.

33

It is love which discriminates between right and wrong, and leads to the gates of God's kingdom.

34

Love is a magic state of being, limitless and without bounds. Love and expand into the infinite.

35

The Light Behind the Form: A Poem

We see the light behind the form

When hate and separate thought subside

Truth glowing after passing storm

Love quieting the raging tide

The love that is the quiet peace

The joy that's known in time and space

The innocence, the trust and faith

He shines through every child's face

So come dear brothers, live the truth

And let the love shine from each heart

So quiet, subtle, undisturbed

For you and He will never part

36

Seeing All within Oneself

The wise man knows he's part of all

The very essence of the call

With conscious knowing he observes

With wonder at His sacred word

We're in the very air we breath

We're in the rocks and in the leaves

And they are within us as well

From tiny wave to largest swell

In everything we play a part

And all in us, from very start

The sacred ripples from His breath

Gives all things life, from birth to death

Sacred music, sacred strings

He strums creating everything

Commanding light to fill the dark

The stars and heavens from one spark

With irresistible command

As ocean waves turn rock to sand

His infinite and perfect plan

Created all. Created man

Who as reflection of above

Who's sacred gift is perfect Love

Vibrations which hold all in place

Reflections of His holy face

37

To The Mothers

Sweet Mother Goddess, pure in heart

You loved us since before the start

You loved us as we learned to fly

We never thought you'd say good by

Always there to catch our fall

To help us conquer any wall

Until we could stand on our own

Until the time came to leave home

And so we journey down the road

You showed the way. You lightened the load

Our time together went so fast

What was once future, now is past

With endless love, yet heavy heart

You watch as precious ones depart

A part of you is always there

There is no weight you cannot bear

A part of you we'll always be

You love us now and endlessly

Always there to help us grow

We feel you close, but do not know

The true depth of the love you hold

A love that never can grow cold

A love that nurtures, lifts and holds

Soft and gentle, yet so bold

You're like a soft still lake at dawn

Yet tempests flare when there's a wrong

For you are beauty, goodness, truth

You're the foundation, walls and roof

Protecting and enriching all

Supporting family, standing tall

Until we could stand on our own

Expressing love as we were shown

As husbands, wives, as parents, friends

The cycle turns, but never ends

And all the love, our mothers shared

We draw upon, we are prepared

To carry the torch a few more laps

With loving grace, until perhaps

One day we'll know our mother's love

So pure and flowing from above

Into our hearts for us to share

Connecting all hearts everywhere

And from above, our mothers know

They shared God's love, maintained the flow

Throughout all history and time

Through mother's love, we touch divine.

38

What is It?

It is fragrant as a spring wind

With colors vivid and alive

It's song gentle and caressing

Yet flowing with immeasurable power

Without beginning, nor end

It is and shall always be

A great truth is concealed within it

A truth known to those who are wise

But veiled from those who have yet to blossom

It is life flowing from its mother's breast

Guided by the spirit behind all

What is it?

It is Love

39

Love

Forever the encourager of life

Behind all that exists

Silent, more subtle than the wind

But the strongest of all that is strong

While touching all, it waits to be touched

Behind the veil of manifestation

Stands Love

The common denominator of the cosmos

Love expresses itself and is directed by itself

It responds only to itself and gives only of itself

Love is complete unto itself.

40

A Meditation Journey For All

Descending into the depths of consciousness, securely fastened to the lifeline of a holy prayer, mantra or seed thought, we enter into the silence, the inner peace within all. Pure and undisturbed is the silence. Peace, beyond description, where thoughts cannot exist, for you are approaching the realm of pure knowing. Go deeper, releasing all contact with the senses. Enter into the ecstasy of sweet communion with spirit, yours and that behind all. In perfect stillness recognize the Causal reality and know you are home. The silence is within all. It has only to be discovered and held sacred within. Upon each return from this knowing, you will become increasingly conscious of the inner beauty, expressing itself through the sacred realm of Peace. Ever conscious of the inner peace, one becomes the wisdom of the Self and His Kingdom becomes established on earth as it is in Heaven.

41

Each of us expresses the whole through a unique individuality reflecting the light of the whole. Know this and let it blaze forth. Clear the way and awaken the sleeper within.

42

By emptying ourselves of our own self will, we become sparkling vessels to hold His essence.

43

I ask the Lord to dwell in me. He answers, "I dwell in all those who have become Love, for by becoming Love, you reclaim your oneness with me."

44

Through Joy

Through Joy we live each day fully.

Through Love we maximize the present.

Through goodness, we attract all that is good to us.

Through being, we become the truth.

Do not fight that which is within you. Neither should you force its opening. Let it bloom like a Lilly in the sun, and your fragrance will draw to you all that you need. Recognize this fact and it will be so, for in truth it already is.

45

Humility and Wisdom

Humility is glimpsed as one begins seeing God's infinite presence in everything and everyone. Wisdom is glimpsed as one begins seeing themselves in everything, and everything in themselves.

46

Within and Without

Peaceful oneness lies within.

Chaos and illusion lies without.

Within we find Love, Virtue and Light.

Without we find the illusion of separateness. False pathways which while pretending to lead to the ultimate, lead only to death.

Beyond thought lies the inner realm, visited only through meditation and sweet communion.

Without, we find duality, the pairs of opposites and the shadows they cast.

Enlightened living melts the shadows and illusions.

Find yourself within, and serve those without, who have not yet learned how to see.

We serve, one encounter at a time.

47

Whispers

Whispers in the twilight, calling unceasingly.

Weeping when not answered. Rejoicing when heard.

Whispers in the silence, calling one home.

They are forever calling, for they are you.

48

Humility and gratitude are inseparable. They are aspects of the same wonder. The wonder of unfoldment.

49

See light and love in all and become the path.

50

Consciousness and Expression

The infinite nature of God is beyond human comprehension, but we can begin to know the Father through the Son, the creative principle. Where Spirit and matter come together there is consciousness which expresses itself through the various forms of creation. The more sophisticated the form the more completely the consciousness, of the One, can express itself. Some feel it is consciousness that shepherds the form of expression through its evolutionary progression, driven by a desire to know itself more intimately. This process is the reassembling of the sacred hologram (*see my book, Water Wisdom - A Journey of Discovery, Chapter 9*), a process that continues throughout eternity until the complete nature and plan of the Father is again revealed and complete.

51

Turning Your Gaze

The experience of life with its trials and successes, joys and sorrows, leads us toward wisdom, but does not reveal it. Experiences, once exhausted, cause one to turn their gaze from the outside world to the world within. It is here where wisdom is revealed and reclaimed as the gift given by the Father before the universe was born.

52

Light and Love does not pour in from without, they pour in from within.

53

Turning within is the process of At-One-Ment, the blissful journey to heaven. Love is our guide. Egoic separation is the chain which holds us from our goal. Detachment and selfless service are the keys which free us from these chains.

54

Judgement and criticism are the great dividers of humanity, yet they are effects and not the cause. The cause behind judgement and criticism is fear. The cure for fear is discovering the truth. The truth is Oneness and Oneness is Love.

55

Find yourself in a truly humble state and you will find you are standing in the light. Recognize Christ in all that exists and you will find that humility has been your bridge to greater understanding.

56

A Question of Flow

Giving is a question of flow. It is the free transfer of loving energy between two or more points of light. We are the points of light.

Attachment, giving with expectation of return, selfishness, judgement, and anger all tend to hinder or disrupt the flow, causing congestions which can manifest as disease, depression and imbalances in life.

True giving is facilitated by knowing that which we really are, and the recognition of it in others. This is the realization of Oneness in all life which wells up as overflowing joy when given selflessly, becoming an eternal spring and bringing life to a barren land.

57

Frustration and Understanding

Frustration is often the result of one or more personalities colliding with other personalities. Understanding and patience are the natural result of one seeing only the Higher Self in others, thus bypassing the sometimes challenged personality.

58

The Eyes of a Child

One cannot commune with the higher during meditation or prayer and then carry on daily actions through the personality (or lower self), and expect to express all that was exchanged during the earlier communion. Instead, see through the eyes of a child. Love, give, and forgive. In this way we become the higher and express more directly through our higher nature.

59

Fear, The False Construct

Fear has no purpose other than that which we give it. It has no power other than that we charge it with. Fear is a false construct. There is no fear in the higher realms. It is a separative phenomenon of the physical world. Examine it closely and the illusion which seems so real soon dissolves in the light of universal truth and service to others.

60

Loving Energy Flows

Beautiful acts and thoughts of service and love cause loving energy flows from God to the area of service. The greater the service, the greater the flow and, as a consequence, the greater the energy available to see clearly and touch the divine. Selfish service causes congestion in the flow, thus reducing the energy or light which enables one to see. Quite literally, those who think or participate in selfish actions live in darkness.

61

Citizens of the Kingdom

We must not wait for someone to make us citizens of the Kingdom of Heaven. We must become citizens by realizing that we are and have always been so. Let the energy of the Father (that in which we live and move and have our being) move through us in selfless giving. The more we give unselfishly and without expectation, the more we become our true selves, that which has always been.

62

Allowing the energy of God to show forth through you is service of the very highest order.

63

Let service be your mantra. Service waits only on intent to move from potential to the present moment.

64

When God is realized, we tap into the unlimited energy resulting from the fusion, into one, of the pairs of opposites, of duality.

65

See the child within yourself. See the child in all people.

AND YOU WILL SEE GOD.

66

Know Yourself

Identify your fears and know they have no place in God's world

Identify your selfish attitudes and habits and know that they are not you

Identify your emotional reactions and know that you are not their servant

Know who you are and be that

You are the very essence of all that is

The star dust which forms your body was drawn together by you yourself

As part of His great Plan

Be that truth

It is up to each of us to choose and actualize our potential

Pierce the veil through pure being

Only illusion stands between us and His reality

67

Serving Spirit

Our physical emotional and mental bodies are the vehicles or tools through which we serve Spirit. We are the conscious essence expressing His Oneness through these tools, these vehicles. Do not make the mistake of identifying with the tools. We are not the tools. We are that which is behind the tools, reflections of the essence of all that is.

68

Gentleness and Passion

Love. Who can adequately describe it? It is so many things. It is life itself. It is the wonder on a child's face. It is a refreshing breeze blowing across fertile lands. It is the beautiful song of a nightingale. It is the gentleness and passion within. Love has infinite faces and manifests through infinite forms. Love is freedom. Love must flow like the wind. Love cannot be held or tethered. For love held in a mold soon crystalizes and decays. Love is energy and energy must flow to be.

69

The Gauntlet Ahead, A Prayer Within

What are the challenges ahead and how shall we know them? Will we have the wisdom to recognize them, the courage to face them, and the love and wisdom to deal with them? Will love be our guide or will fear and anger move our hand, before higher sensibilities are evoked and become our shepherd. Will we be able to meet each rebuke with kindness, each slight with lovingness, each difference of opinion with patience and understanding. Will we have the strength to serve Spirit when the whole world calls for its surrender. Will we follow truth unerringly, or will we succumb to convenient rationalization, procrastination and laziness?

- Oh Lord we pray for your light and love. Let it be our guide. Let it move us, even as the wind moves the branches of the forest trees. Let love find us worthy that it becomes our constant companion and guide, always leading us to do your Will.

- "Make us an instrument of thy peace." (*Saint Francis*). Help us to empty ourselves, that you might fill us.

- Cleanse that which veils your truth. Project your light on fear that it might be seen for the illusion that it is. Give us the light and wisdom that we might serve within your great design, and courage that we might succeed in your service. Purify us so that you are no longer hidden from our sight. Fill us with forgiveness, love, compassion, and sacrifice.

- Lift us unto thy sacred feet.

70

When self-will is no more, we are like a harp in His hands and beauty is its music.

71

Confidence is not a cause. Confidence is an effect, the radiation from one who knows who he or she is, and can remain focused in the Truth.

72

Friends or Pretenders

Ego and self-will; how they torment us while feigning friendship. Emphasizing the false desires of the personality, they cast a shadow upon the truth, hiding it from our view, all in the name of protecting us. Freeing oneself from their grasp is the key to returning home. Knowing the truth of who we really are soon dissolves them into the nothingness from which they came. Remove the ego and Christ will return to the throne within, a throne he never really left. His grace is a gift, but it must be accepted before received.

73

Becoming

The process of becoming is realizing the truth of I Am. It is a joyful beingness, not really a process, but a fact; not so much a journey, but rather an emergence. Not the gaining of knowledge, but a knowing. Not a surprise, but a natural awakening. The process of becoming is a choice which becomes a demand, for it was and is and always will be truth. It is there in front of us. We have only to reach our hand. *CHOOSE IT.*

74

The Greatest Gift of All

Just as the sun sustains all life within its ocean of energetic light, warmth and energy, so we must give freely. We do this by choosing to express His endless compassionate beingness into the world, freely and without expectation of return. A life of giving unselfishly is a life well lived. Such a life is on the path, the stream of love energy flowing from the Father and ultimately back to Him. Giving is like turning on an electrical switch. Nothing flows when it is off. We feel separate and alone. But when on, the flow is endless, continuous and unlimited. The greatest gift of all is the gift of yourself. This includes the gift of love, understanding, guidance, patience and time. This is the gift of virtuous example. The disciple's example, when true, pure and unwavering is the greatest gift of all. Christ said, "I am the way." He laid his life down for those he loved and the world has never been the same.

75

Soul-Centered

True humility is the recognition of oneness with the Great Soul behind all that is. Ego melts in the light of this truth. One puts off the trappings of self-centeredness and puts on the robe of Soul-centeredness. Faith and right action bring us to this doorway, to revelation. This door is opened not by pushing or raising, but by our becoming the door. We do not step through to revelation, we become revelation. Just like the Great One before us, we 'become the way.' The truth is, you have always been so. It was just temporarily hidden from your earthly eyes.

76

Leave Regret Behind

Do not focus on the sadness and injustice of the crucifixion. Rather dwell deeply on the wonder of His resurrection and the joy of His loving presence within you and within all. Positive thoughts illuminate the pathway home. Negative thoughts line the pathway to hell and sadness. Leave regret behind, for it does not serve you. Let your love shine forth and heal all from within.

77

And So We Travel On

And so we travel on. Accelerating, while not moving, for we travel in the infinite potential of the silence which touches all simultaneously. Know it to be so and it is so. Quiet the unruly mind and reach into the depths of unlimited wisdom. Know always that the heart knows the way. Serve the heart and realize that in so doing you are serving all.

78

There Is A Way

The **way** is meditation and prayer which leads us back into the light. Gradually we become accustomed again to the innocent blazing beauty which was present at birth, but slowly was veiled from our view by earthly illusions, as we grew to adulthood. This is the innocent beauty that can be seen in the light of every child's face. We can find it again. We can become it again. It is not gone, just hidden. As our memory is restored through meditation and prayer, it soon is reflected in every aspect of our lives, carried as a shining torch. The light shines within us, through us, and all around us, for we have remembered who we are.

79

"He is wise who remains focused in me. Make every act an offering to me. Make every thought a gift to me." (Krishna addressing Arjuna in the Bhavagad Gita)

80

The Great Man

The great man dies, the people mourn.

But when alive, his truth they scorn.

They knew it to be true and right.

But unaccustomed to the light,

The messenger is shouted down.

His message jeered because the sound,

Is painful to the profane ear.

Yet, something deep begins to stir.

The message is not lost but grows.

 Into the world the message flows.

The song is sung, where Christ calls home.

And then the harbinger is gone.

His body shed, but truth remains.

It lives within to cleanse the stains,

Of mortal thought and mortal fear.

To help the deaf begin to hear.

81

The Bliss of Life

The bliss of life flows to those who love unceasingly and without expectation; Those who have become the greatest by becoming the least; Those who are a light unto the world. These become love itself by realizing that it has always been.

82

Joy is the natural result of a growing awareness into the oneness of life.

83

Heavenly Treasures

Do not wish for freedom from this life in order to find heaven in the next, for we are eternal beings and carry our heavenly treasures within us, every step we take, forever and ever. Heaven calls to a loving heart, revealing itself, sharing its treasures, and granting access into its bliss now and today and forever. We have but to look and it is there.

84

Right Here, Right Now

See all as beloved brothers and sisters, mothers and fathers, sons and daughters. See the innocence in all, so often hidden by the perceived trials of this world. See yourself in everything and everything within yourself. This is the way of wisdom, which resides in heaven, right here and right now.

85

Laugh in the Face of Adversity

When the world slings its spears and arrows at you, realize that it is an opportunity to move closer to the Father. Rejoice, for our purpose in this life is to return to our roots, our roots in heaven. Laugh in the face of adversity, for it has no power over you. You can only do your best, and all is for the Father.

86

It is how we perceive the world that gives it its texture. We can choose to see our daily activities as drudgery, or we can choose to see them as a gift.

87

See all as a gift and the veil, which once blinded you, will lift from your eyes. Perform all obligations with joy and the world has no choice but to love you and to follow your example.

88

Many Paths, One Destination

Remember that each of us is at a slightly different place on the continuum of understanding leading back to Spirit. When we truly hear God's call, our path is a straight line directly to spirit. I can't ask you to come over to my spot and then we will travel to Spirit together. The shortest path is always a direct line from wherever each of us is. This is why they say there are as many paths to spiritual awakening as there are travelers on the path.

89

Once the call is heard, all paths lead to the exact same endpoint.

90

I like to think of each path as a silky thread of light. Together they create a beautiful tapestry of light blending heaven and earth.

91

In truth, awakening is a journey taken without moving, for when we are awake we realize that we are everywhere and always continuously and simultaneously.

92

When the world around you appears hopelessly lost, surround it with your love and continue to dance. The rest will take care of itself.

93

The Sacred Cause

Beyond the forms of this existence, beyond the energy which gives animation to the inanimate, beyond all thoughts, lies the sacred Cause, the universal Mind, that which connects all, that which we call God, the Sacred One, the Father, Holy Spirit, Love, Christ, Buddha, Allah. The Sacred Cause has infinite names. All are symbols of the Truth which initiated all and flows through all. Yet these symbols touch only an infinitesimally small fragment of the essence we call, the Creator.

94

Love flows in whatever measure we give it. We are the only limiting factor.

95

Seamless Oneness

When you Love, serve and forgive, a larger life will present itself to you. Clear vision reveals that it is a life shared with all. A loving heart reaches out to all like a beacon recognizing and embracing all as its own. There is no separation. There never was. Only seamless oneness connecting all with all.

96

The Great Manipulator

The illusion of fear is the great manipulator deftly used by those who worship dominance and control, to further their agenda. Do not let fear move you to action or cause you to withdraw into inaction. Follow your heart for the pathway through 'the valley of the shadow of death,' was written on every atom of your being at the beginning of time.

97

Our Natural State

Quiet the mind.

Set the personality, the small self aside.

Let the light of Love bathe you.

Feel it around you and within you,

Like a limitless spring of fresh vitalizing water

Feel the flow.

Feel the warmth of its light.

Know it as the center of your essence,

Then send it out into the world with an endless and effortless loving attitude of giving.

This completes the circuit and makes you whole.

This is your natural state.

98

An Instant of Clarity

Awakening is not the "I" becoming one with the Universal Soul. It is the "I" recognizing that it was never separate from the Universal Soul; that any differentiation was part of its own self manifested illusion.

Yes, we are in contact with this illusion through our physical form, our bodies, but the truth behind this appearance is never separate. This cannot easily be grasped since our contact and communication with the world is through our senses which recognize only physical phenomenon. Yet in deep contemplation we touch the true essence and motivating, or causal force, behind all that is.

It begins with intense one-pointed concentration which quiets the mind. Only when the mind is quiet will the essence behind all rise to the surface and reveal itself. This is the level of contemplation.

The mind is still. It is not active at this level, yet all is revealed in an instant of clarity. When we touch this knowing, we feel like we have awakened from a great dream. This is the goal. Meditation is the key.

99

Find the Quiet

It is when we are in touch with the quiet place within that we truly serve, for our conscious contact with this higher truth enables it to flow into the world. We become conduits through which the world is reminded of its true nature.

- Know this and do not be deferred from the quest of finding the quiet. In time it becomes your natural state and the miracles of His kingdom will be revealed through holy wisdom. All the miracles performed by Christ are small compared to the impact of the truth which constantly flowed and flows through Him to humanity. This is how we can serve most effectively, even in the midst of the world's confusion.

- Find the quiet. Carry it with you and lead all you touch to the 'Still Waters' of His realm. In this natural and beautiful way, we heal the world. In this way we serve. Those we encounter will feel the energy of the Quiet and be compelled through ancient memory to find it in themselves for it is their true essence also.

- And so it spreads its unending salvation. And so His Kingdom is reestablished on earth as in heaven.

100

I Am the Wind

God's breath gives me life

It is his gift to all.

It awakens the sleeper within.

It opens us to His conscious being.

The wind caresses us like a loving mother,

Cooling, refreshing, and nurturing our growing awareness.

His breath lights all creation.

His breath is the expansion and contraction of all.

It is life itself.

It is the Holy Spirit.

That which inspires all existence, all forms.

It is All.

In the silence it soon is clear

I am the breath of life.

I am the wind.

101

Silently Singing

Quiet beauty, silently singing

Deep within calling to me

Joyous bells silently ringing

Inviting all to come and to be

Peace, peace calling me home

Silently calling so endlessly

Letting me know, I'm not alone

Helping me calm, all raging seas

Love, love, silently showing

Lighting the way which sets us all free

Soon, soon, all will be knowing

Chaos replaced by pure harmony

102

Love must first be recognized within, before it can be recognized without.

103

Do not identify with the form. Do not identify with the material. Identify with the Cause behind the form.

104

Prayer is more effective when we pray **with** God, then when we pray **to** God, for the Father knows all needs. If we are to rise above the world's illusion, we must unite with the Father and soar with his wings, knowing they are also our wings.

105

Ever Growing Echoes

When we look upon or think about something loved, that love is always reflected back to us in ever growing echoes of joy. Love in its infinite expressions is the only thing in the world of value. Loving is the only action in the world of value, and being Loved is the only goal in the world of value. Worldly diversions try to draw us away from this quest, yet it remains the only true quest. Love, and all you do say or think will have value. Be love and become that which humanity has searched for since the fall.

106

When we live a loving life in the present, the past fades from its position of influence, while the future is made perfect by the guidance of the Now.

107

When we build the bridge between the higher and the lower, consciousness reunites and is again whole.

108

The Inadequacy of Words

Words fall woefully short of adequately describing higher principals, for words are of the world and, until His Kingdom and Earth are reunited, words vibrate at a level too low to carry the full light from above.

Do not let this concern you. They are only words and unable to convey what the higher Self already knows. Rather turn to love. It will reveal all heavenly secrets without words and you will begin to glimpse the majesty of the Father.

109

The Journey Towards Understanding

The pathway home is Love as is the goal at the end of the path. It is a journey towards understanding. Understanding which is written within our hearts and every vibration comprising our being. Love is the key to unlocking the mystery, a mystery misplaced eons ago and now calling to be found anew.

110

From, Through and To

The journey home is a journey from Love, through Love, and to Love. Love is its beginning ending and all that is between. When we reach the end of the journey we realize that we never really left. We realize that we have arrived back at the beginning.

111

Guidance

I ask for guidance to be the peacemaker my heart longs for. Deep in the silence I hear, "Choose." For each of us has been given the gift of free will. As His command reverberates within my being, I soon realize that it is not enough to say the words or think the thoughts. Rather, we must have an overpowering conviction to become who we really are, to become the truth so completely that every molecule of our being sings its song, sharing it with all and healing the world.

112

The Diamond Within

The search is for our Christhood, the Holy Grail against which all else pales, a journey which all must take and complete. It is the diamond within, waiting patiently for its light to be freed from egoic diversions and illusions.

- Angels whisper in our ears that it resides in the heart, a priceless pearl of indescribable beauty. We have only to find it and in so doing release it from its bonds.

- As we chased the desires of the world we lost sight of it. What is it, you wonder?

- It is the innocence with which we came into the world and upon successful completion of life's journey will leave this world with. Love is the path. The world is the training ground through which we must pass. As realization evolves, love becomes the wings on our feet, lifting us high above the apparent obstacles of the world. Love is all, the lesson and the goal. Through Love we know the Father, for they are one and the same. Become Love and realize your connection and oneness with All.

- Initially, the seeking requires faith, but as Love lifts us higher and our vision becomes clear, faith will be replaced with knowing and knowing with being.

113

Gratitude

Thank you for loving us so much that we can touch you by touching Love, for you are Love.

I choose Love, for only by loving am I complete. When I reach for you, thank you for reaching back.

Thank you for waiting patiently for us to look up and take your outstretched hand.

Only by loving are we complete. Only by giving can we get close to you. Only through unselfish living can we grow into our inheritance.

I ask my outward personality to stand aside. It has been a faithful companion, but I am not it.

I am Love. That is all I am, and yet it is everything.

114

Reach Higher

When life mistreats, you feel alone

When darkness seems to freely roam

Gaze upward and behold your home

Reach Higher

See endless heaven in your heart

The love inside will never part

Emblazoned there, till end, from start

Reach higher

See His perfection in the trees

In birds and flowers, humming bees

The gentle caress of the breeze

Reach higher

For it resides in all you see

In all you hear and touch and feel

In giving and a smiles appeal

Reach higher

It's always there, a part of all

It picks you up from every fall

It stretches you to make you tall

Reach higher

Through endless journey, it is there

Supporting you to help you bear

A gift while climbing heavens stair

Reach higher

For there's no limit to one's growth

No meets and bounds, no castle moat

Turn to the light, sing through His throat

Reach higher

And soon you'll see with open eyes

And know the secrets of the wise

That which you are, begins to rise

Reach higher

All that you see, reflects this truth

Hidden from the profane, uncouth

The secret of eternal youth

Reach higher

And so now take the lessons learned

From darkness, now to heaven turned

The truth revealed like butter churned

Reach higher

No longer lost, we hold His light

The way back home, revealed bright

The blind have now regained their sight

Reach higher

So now awake, renew the quest

Hearts beat anew within each chest

He only ask we do our best

Reach higher

115

A Pilgrims Journey

Refrain:
Searching far and wide for treasure
Chasing all on earth that shines
Diamonds, gems and earthly pleasures
He is lost among and vines
Endless hunger burns within him
From the pain he seeks release
Till the guide inside reminds him
Search the heart to find true peace

What here follows is a story,
Of a man who traveled far.
This a story with a message.
Offered as a guiding star.

Message herein for the searchers.
Those who hear the sacred song.
Those who long to find the treasure,
Awakening from sleep so long.

Hear the song of endless calling.
Calling to the children lost
Calling with healing forgiveness.
Find it, no matter the cost.

Mystery, the sacred music,
Must be solved to wake from sleep.
Oh, his heart longs for the secret.
Must reach out, to those that weep.

Maybe truths around the corner.
Maybe riches, maybe power.
Maybe a new gem that sparkles.
He must find it, now's the hour.

Maybe chasing all that's shiny.
Maybe that's the answer sought.
He will press on and soon conquer,
All that binds him, every knot.

For his earthly will is powerful.
Focused mind should soon achieve.
He will press on, nothing stops him.
He will win the prize he seeks.

Decades pass and he's successful,
At obtaining worldly wealth.
Wealthy beyond his consumption.
Wealth that only leads to death.

And his heart still feels so empty.
Has he led himself astray?
Has he wasted precious moments?
Is this one big masquerade?

And from deep within a murmur.
Faintly heard through aching heart.
Child, your longing's misdirected,
Chasing all that shines on earth.

This a recipe for sadness.
Which can never fill the void.
You're a child of Love's perfection.
Manifested love and joy.

The truth lies within your being.
Look within to find the truth.
You reside within the infinite.
Not the matrix, you call earth.

For a moment, he could feel it.
Loving wisdom filling him.
It was just a flash in silence.
In that flash, a holy hymn.

Just a flash, but something touched him,
Well beyond his earthly life.
Images from silent knowing.
Sacred path past earthly strife.

Where to look, he starts to ponder.
How to find that healing light.
Longs to feel that warm completeness.
Longs to make his mis-steps right.

So, he searched with endless effort,
Endless research, endless leads.
Answers just around the corner.
Prepare the earth and plant the seeds

Endlessly, acquired knowledge,
Books and writings, he absorbed.
But his heart ached in the silence.
Nothing seemed to fill the void.

Knowledge too, was a possession.
Just more things, which weighed him down.
Maybe this is not the answer.
Maybe this is not the crown?

Perhaps wise ones could direct him.
Perhaps a guru or a preacher.
Surely, they will have the answer.
Surely one could be his teacher.

So, in search, again he traveled.
He crossed the path of many wise.
Many that were false, misleading.
Very few could open eyes.

But then one rose above others.
Looking kindly on the man.
With a look of knowing, uttered.
Look inside for sacred land.

No one in your steps can travel.
Only you can walk your road.
Each of us uniquely journeys,
At your birth was this bestowed.

Listen to your heart which calls you.
Know it as your very own.
Feel the bliss and know with confidence,
You are on the pathway home.

No one else but you can find it.
Each uniquely knows the way.
Follow love inside which guides you.
Through your love turn night to day.

With these words the teacher left him.
With a tear, he turned to say.
Love inside will never fail you.
Inward journey is the way.

Robert H. Wellington

All alone he sat and pondered.
Oh, so close and yet so far.
Sitting there, the silence saw him.
Soon dispelling his despair.

Comforting, it whispered softly.
Look within and I will share.
With internal contemplation,
You will find the golden stair.

In the silence, he found loving,
Thoughts of family and of friends.
Thoughts connecting, all existing.
Filling all the voids within.

Healing wounds, so long he carried.
False companions, held so dear.
Now were gone, replaced by silence.
On his cheek a lonely tear.

Peace beyond all comprehension.
All potential within reach.
New acceptance and forgiveness,
Replaying the wise one's speech.

Had he found that something special?
Had he found the chalice lost?
Sitting there his eyes now opened.
With new vision now, he saw.

So much clarity and knowing.
So much love had set him free.
He sat there for countless moments.
Restless mind, now quiet sea.

Thoughts of family soon awoke him.
Once was shackled, now he's free.
Must serve all, in joy's communion.
Serving is the sacred key.

Finding love within he traveled,
Near and far to share the word.
Awakening that something special.
In all met upon the road.

Knowing now the truths within him.
Veiled until Love's inflamed.
Love that's shared without an effort.
Love once lost but now reclaimed.

Those encountered, feel that special,
Energy that's from the All.
Energy that Love inspires.
Resurrecting those that fall.

The true healer knows the secret.
He's the instrument, not the cure.
Choosing to let God flow through him.
Healing all and making pure.

We are vessels for His glory.
Yet He longs for us to know.
Our true kinship as His body.
Sacred oneness with God's flow.

With that thought wisdom awakens.
Blindness now is perfect sight.
Knowing truth resides within him,
In his heart he holds it tight.

Though the ego begs to differ.
Working hard to claim its place.
"I was there when you were single."
"When alone you faced disgrace."

But the light of truth shines on it.
Yes, my friend you played a roll.
Now let go and be a witness.
To the truth that makes one whole.

In the light, the ego softened.
For it too began to see.
All we meet upon the journey.
Play a part in Love's great play.

Slowly fading from existence.
Knowing that it played its role.
Farewell to an old companion,
Diamond now where once was coal.

So, the truth does not reside in,
Things that do not dwell within.
Neither guru's, will, nor treasures,
Can the emptiness, they fill.

This he gives to those that follow.
Stepping through the curtain tear.
Use it as you will my family.
It is here for all to share

Refrain:
Searching far and wide for treasure
Chasing all on earth that shines
Diamonds, gems and earthly pleasures
He was lost among and vines
Endless hunger burns within him
From the pain he seeks release
Till the guide inside reminds him
Search the heart to find true peace

116

More on Time

Before creation there was no time, only timelessness. It seems that time appeared with creation, for before creation all was liquid peace with no movement or vibratory awareness against which time could measure. When the One Creator said, "Let there be light," all appeared and with it time. Was time an after-thought or was it a natural biproduct of manifestation? Could the One have just as easily said, "Let there be time," and light and creation would naturally manifest? Think about it. Time is the dimension which is charged with relating one vibratory manifestation to every other vibratory manifestation, or one physical body to all others. Thus, time without creation cannot exist. Can creation exist without time? All creation is manifested and held together by vibratory interaction. Vibration by its very nature is based on movement and where there is movement, there is time. Thus, time and creation cannot exist without each other. They are intimately related, like two sides of the same coin.

Transcending time requires an intense knowing and becoming of universal oneness, which I would liken to a loving intensity beyond human ability to fully grasp. But that doesn't preclude us from touching it in profound ways during meditation, contemplation and prayer. Only through Love does time give way to Joy. The pain of watching time seemingly slip away, is replaced by the bliss of growing through Joy. When one meditates on oneness, he/she will find a peaceful consciousness and an accompanying stability of mind which slows time itself. Only through this experience does man know its peace, and through peace, revelation.

Many would say that merging into oneness is the ultimate human experience in this body. In many ways, merging in oneness is the traversing of the bridge between spirit (or 5th dimensional man) and man of the 3D world. At the apex of the rainbow bridge, man finds himself with one foot in heaven and one foot still on earth. One more step and the pilgrim merges into the surrendering perfection of the divine mind, the home left long ago. Of course, one must travel far beyond 5th density before knowing the Creator perfectly, but this is the threshold between the physical and spirit worlds. Taking this last step requires total surrender. The nectar of spirit can only be tasted by surrendering to the loving embrace of that which has been waiting patiently throughout the ages for the return of its Prodigal sons and daughters. We must let go of the world to take these last steps into Gods outstretched arms.

This is our Holy Grail, our quest, and our Soul's deepest desire.

117

In a very real sense, we are the authors of the infinite secrets we long to discover.

118

The infinite names for God reside in infinity, which is the pilgrims true home.

119

You seemingly journey to the end point, only to discover it is the place from which you started.

120

There is not one member of the human race that we do not know on a higher level.

121

Energy by itself, without guidance is just energy. Energy directed by loving intent is the servant and partner of the Divine.

122

Love provides the grid or template through which energy flows as it dances with creation, perfectly reflecting the divine plan. Thus we must constantly Love so that God's kingdom is realized on earth.

123

It Is In Loving That We Are Loved
(St. Francis)

We know love by loving.

We experience love only when we love.

We choose love by loving.

We become love by loving.

It is a choice given to each of us at the beginning of time.

It is that easy.

It is that hard.

124

Oh glorious day. Oh dance of ages. Oh loving hands forever ready to assist. How can we repay you for removing the veils from our eyes? How can we thank you for letting us see?

125

Children

What precious gifts. Given by the Creator to be cherished, loved and guided until the cycle begins anew when they have children of their own. A loving parent sees heaven through the eyes of their children. At that moment of communion the child also sees Heaven's perfect reflection through the eyes of the parent. In this way we guide each other on the pathway home. We teach our children how to live in this world while not losing their spiritual balance. Likewise, their close proximity to heaven reminds us of our true nature and points the way as we leave this world behind at the end of this journey, and follow our divine song. We were here to hold the light for them and assist them on their journey home. Likewise they remind us of our intimate relationship to the One. It is an endless cycle with each generation playing their critical role as together we travel the narrow path back to the Father.

126

Looking and Seeing

Looking and seeing Love in all things; Knowing through our higher awareness that Love is within us and all. Communing with Love every minute of the day and night. Becoming Love increasingly with each thought, word, and action. This is our quest. This is our destiny. Turn inward and you will know.

127

The act of giving without expectation fills us with the Holy Spirit. Spiritual progress is made when we are lovingly able to give unceasingly. The mystery is that no matter how much is given, always we receive more in return.

It is His law. It is His gift.

128

A Prayer

Oh Heavenly Father, help those who search for their life's work to find it.

Help those who have found it to complete it.

Open our hearts and minds that they are forever turned towards you.

Bathe us in the rays of your loving goodness, that we may blossom like the lotus.

Let your beauty and fragrance radiate through us, that we may draw others to you.

Charge us with your Holy Spirit that we may charge others as your ambassadors.

And bless and protect the children through whom you remind us of your constant presence.

129

The Pathway Home

Behind the physical, behind the personality and false ego lies the Soul, the perfect reflection of the Father. Each of us during incarnation is trying our best, with various degrees of success, to bring that perfect reflection to earth, "as it is in Heaven." The challenges of this density often plays havoc with our best intentions, however, and we sometimes get lost temporarily in our own blindness. During times like these our quest can require a heavy dose of forgiveness, both for others and for ourselves, followed by efforts to purify our physical and emotional vehicles, our very essence, so that we can again hear the song of the heavenly host calling us home.

We have only to hear it for a moment and we will regain our foothold on the narrow path back to the Father. Seek the guidance of prayer, meditation, contemplation and right action, and spirit will straighten your path's winding way, and put the wind at your back. Actions, words and thoughts so guided always lead to the One, and His perfect plan is restored with each step we take home. It is His promise and His gift. It is our greatest service.

130

Surrender

Some wise ones have said that surrender is the last great choice on the pilgrims pathway home. Such a simple concept. Such a complete and comprehensive thought and action. Without surrender there is no awakening, for only the Lord can awaken and He cannot reside within unless invited. This invitation is evidenced by a total surrender of our little will to His. The strength of the Father comes to us when we have emptied and purified the vessel which is our true self. Then he will sweep into the vacuum and fill us with his essence. But He will not come before this no matter how much we pray. Prayer without surrender is not heard. It cannot be acted on. It is His will which makes all things right again and our surrender or choice, is required for His will to be established on earth. Freedom of choice is His great gift to us; The choice to love him and bring him into our lives, the choice to make him central in all our activities, the freedom to live life more abundantly.

131

Completely Let Go

To go deeper in meditation, let God's hand guide you. Completely let go. Completely surrender. The temptation is so overwhelming, and apparently natural, to try to guide the process. Yet this arrests the meditation experience and the aspirant's progress. Trust and have faith that if you let go, he will catch you and carry you to the highest realms.

132

Walking With God

When all within becomes light

Then one walks in holiness

When Joy is the only medium of expression

Then one walks as one with God

133

The Same Love

When you feel love, whether it be for a family member, nature, or the joy of life, you are feeling the presence of God. You are communing with God. You are drawing on the one true principle. Know it is the same love, whether you feel it or someone else feels it. It is the oneness behind all life. There is no separation of the true Self with the true Principle. We and all that exists are one family. Although the physical world appears to the worldly senses to be separate, know that the essence behind all creation is One.

134

Fear of the Now

It seems we are afraid of the Now,

Preferring instead to dwell in the past,

And worry about the future.

Yet the Now is the point of peace and equilibrium within each of us,

A point we each share.

Knowing this is half the battle toward the light.

The other half is overcoming the fears

Which keep us from the pure joy of Now.

135

All that is good and beautiful is Spirit expressing its perfect nature.

Observe beauty and know that you are communing with Spirit.

136

Breath and Will

I breath in and God fills my very being.

I breath out and share His love with all encountered.

On each inbreath, He nourishes me,

On each outbreath, I do His will.

137

I honor the God in myself by honoring the God in others.

I honor the God in others by honoring the God in myself.

138

Tat Tvam Asi

"I am that." "That thou art." "I am that I am."

The sacred and intimate relationship between the individual and the Absolute.

Such a simple phrase. Such an awesome revelation of ultimate truth.

139

Beneath

Beneath the rising and falling thoughts which flow endlessly across the screen of perception.

Beneath the physical manifestation that the wise recognize as their earthly self,

Beneath the actions and thoughts that fill each day,

Resides that which is true and good, timeless and forever.

140

Joy Is Forever

Joy is the nectar of divinity. Joy is forever ours when we accept it from the hands of Spirit and then let it flow freely to all we encounter. The magic is in the sharing, for endless amounts of joy flow in, as one let's it flow to others.

141

Food For Thought

"There was never a time when I was not, nor you, nor these leaders of men. Nor will come a time when we will all cease to be." Bhagavad Gita.

142

All Is Eternal

Our senses recognize only that which is of the world, but our heart knows of other realms. Listen to the heart. Develop your heart sense. Let it guide you and you will never go astray. Lead with the Heart and remember that the mind, though an ally, is always the servant of the Heart.

143

Only You: A Prayer

God bless the journey all are taking with me.

God bless my family and friends,

Co-workers, known and not yet known.

God bless those whom I do not see,

But are there lifting me when I fall.

Thank you for blessing this life and,

Filling it with your abundance and Love.

Help each of us to know you more perfectly each day,

Until the glorious revelation when there is only you.

144

The Perfect Gift

God's perfect gift is the gift of giving. As we give, more is received. It is His gift to both giver and receiver. His kingdom is built on Love and Love grows through giving. Giving and receiving expand into the infinite immediately. There is no hesitation. God gives to us holding nothing back, and has gifted to each of us the ability to do the same. Baptized in His infinite expression we know Him and we realize our intimate connection with Him and All. Go and share all of your Love, for it can only be experienced and enjoyed by giving.

145

Giving and loving are so intertwined as to be inseparable from each other. They are two aspects of the same thing, different folds within the same cloth.

146

Truly knowing the love that we are, is the faith that moves mountains.

147

It is not the 'I' becoming one with the universal Soul, that is enlightenment. It is the 'I' realizing that it was never separate.

148

Separateness

Separateness is the child of our own self-manifested illusion. We appear to be in contact with this illusion through our physical bodies, but in truth, we are never separate. This is hard to grasp by the conscious mind, since all our contact with the physical plane is through our five senses and these recognize only physical phenomenon. Although not available to the five senses, we can touch the true essence and motivating energy behind all that is, in deep contemplation. It begins with intense concentration and meditative stillness. This alone cannot reveal the truth, but it does quiet the mind and, in time, allows a deeper sense to rise to the surface and reveal a deeper truth. This is the level of contemplation. Contemplation opens the door to the higher mind. The physical mind is not active at this level, yet all is known in an instant of clarity. When we touch this knowing, we feel as if awakened from a deep sleep wherein our life has been but a dream. This is the goal we strive for. A loving heart, concentration, meditation and ultimately contemplation are the keys to finding it.

149

The Breath

I am the breath, the expansion and contraction of all creation.

"I am" the breath of life traveling on the wind.

"I am" the breath that gives life to all.

"I am" the breath that gives creation consciousness.

"I am" the breath and the breath is creation.

150

One With the Breezes

We are one with the breezes. Know this when the winds caress you like a loving mother. Know this as you are touched by the light of the sun which drives the winds, whose light flows across endless space joining with all light. Know that behind this light is the energy of His breath which first put creation into motion so long ago; The dreamer of all things, whose very breath is the expansion and contraction of all that exists. It is His breath that swept up matter and gave it life. It is His breath that allows you to know creation as he knows you and all the manifest and unmanifest. Know you are His very breath and soar on His wings.

151

A Simple Truth

Without His Spirit I am empty.

He is the joy which graces my life.

He is the happiness on my children's faces.

He is the beauty in nature.

He is my inspiration.

He is the Love which bonds.

He is the friendship in my relationships.

He is all that is good, beautiful and righteous.

Knowing this is Joy.

Living this is pure inspiration.

Being this leads unerringly to his sacred feet.

152

The Father gives each of us the energy we need to find Him. We have only to choose.

153

Love is both the guide and the path unto His sacred feet.

154

A life without Love is like a ship without a rudder.

155

Between All Thoughts

Between all thoughts, in perfect silence we find you. In the quiet of your holy center you have waited throughout eternity to welcome each of us as we complete the journey home. Only our love and perfection can enter the silence. All worldly baggage has been left behind. Merging with the silence we again become One with you. You are sublime love and in the process of the journey home we have found that perfect vibration and merged with your heart. We have again become your sons and daughters and have taken our place beside you to hold the light for those not yet home.

156

The Guide Within

Each of us has within, a guide, who enables us to see the light, interpret it, and bring it into our daily life. We find it within our heart. Our guide's judgement is without flaw. Sadly, we often ignore the wisdom of this inner guide. We look so desperately outside of ourselves for guidance that we are easily manipulated.

Turn your gaze inward. There is only one guide. In truth it is our very essence, our true self, inseparable from the Father. It's wisdom is the same within each of our hearts. Find it and you will never be led astray by those who need to manipulate. The truth is within us. It is written on our hearts but not in words for words cannot express the infinite. It is written in the loving language of His wisdom. Find the perfect discrimination within, and you will know God.

157

Musings on The Infinite Nature of the Creator

When all was an infinite point of unlimited potential and the circle of creation around the point, had not yet manifested from the mind of the One, there was only I Am. When the infinite One, for whom no name can encompass, released its perfect idea into the void, all creation presented itself to the infinite continuum, waiting only on time for each vibratory expression from the word of the One, to manifest. The One, or God, is the infinite Cause motivating the infinite perfect Idea which is creation, and although infinite, it is an infinitesimally small part of the One. So what is beyond our infinite manifestation? What is beyond our universe?

Mathematically, nothing is beyond the infinite, and yet, perhaps God's math has another dimension, a more profound and mysterious calculus? In fact, it appears that scientists and mathematicians today are making a strong case for the concept of a Multi-Verse. This multiverse is comprised of potentially an unlimited number of universes across dimensions. But to my mind, the concept of a multiverse begs the follow on question, "What is beyond the multiverse?" It is a great mystery, waiting only for the Cause behind All to again breath upon the still waters of infinite potential and create the infinite beyond the infinite.

158

Infinite Beyond the Infinite

My mind wonders at the mystery of an infinite beyond the infinite. In silent moments, flashes of its presence tease my deepest awareness, but do not reveal its secrets. I long for understanding and am answered by the question, "If God is infinite, doesn't it follow that the God/Goddess/All-That-Is would require an infinite playground. And within that infinite playground wouldn't He/She/All desire intelligent playmates, and through 'Freedom of Choice' grant them infinite ways to express themselves while experiencing His creation?"

And so He does.

And so it is.

159

Continued Musings on His Infinite Nature

God longs to express His infinite loving nature. Love must be given to flow and must flow to exist. God needs His creation, in all its essence and permutations, to express His infinite Love through. Love not shared becomes nothing. If God must give Love for love to exist, can we do less.

160

More on the Mystery of Creation

God created us as part of a mysterious plan which one day will be revealed. He gifted us with an overwhelming desire to know Him, a desire which is of Him, and also burns in his own being. It is a beautiful thought that He longs to know us as intensely as we long to know Him. Perhaps as we grow, he grows in some mysterious way. They say that Angels sing with joyful ecstasy whenever a Son of God is born. Has God sent a small part of Himself into the world so that He, along with us, could rediscover, experience and enjoy His glory, through the Son, in an ever increasing symphony of loving expression?

161

Always Present

Always present, it sings it's song, yet, most cannot hear. Spiritual evolution is the process of raising our inner song, our inner vibration to that of Spirit. Then, all He has shared with the wind, is shared freely with us. It resides in the peace found within. There we are lifted to the heights of His perfect expression and become one with it. Not by a new revelation do we become one, but buy recognizing that His song is also our song, and has been since the beginning of time.

162

Let your light illuminate the pathway home. See the glow of the footsteps left behind by those who went before. See the glow of your own footsteps left for those who follow.

163

The magic and mystery of the words which point toward heaven are encrypted at a holy frequency which is only unlocked by a pure seeker who resonates at the same level.

164

Between

Between the thoughts.

Between the words.

Between, the actions,

You will find His Holy Realm.

Here the noise of the world cannot enter.

Here rests the cradle and throne of

Beauty, goodness, truth and joy,

Which heals the world of misguided choices,

As it creates new perfection for consciousness to explore.

Quiet the mind and know this place,

For it is your true home

Tat Tvam Asi

165

Strive to be a clear lens through which the Father's light can shine upon the world.

166

When the you and me within becomes 'I am', then you will truly dance.

167

See, Hear and Know

See God in everything and you will never be alone.

Hear Him in all things and you will never be without song.

Know Him in all and you will be filled in ways unimaginable.

Do His will, which is to Love, and His Joy will embrace,

Every action you take,

Every thought you think,

Every word you utter.

168

Forgiveness and understanding travel together. Both are enhanced by patience. None can exist without Love.

169

Never Forget Who You Are

Sing your song continuously.

Sing it in the silence of morning.

Sing it from the mountain top at high noon.

Sing it in inspiration at sunset.

Sing unceasingly, for you are a child of God and your recognition, your choice, allows him to work through you.

Sing and know you are an integral piece of His plan.

Sing and know that you are loved.

170

Finding the Om Within

Express Love with gratitude

And passionate attitude

With infinite latitude

You'll find your way home

Through Love re-awaken

Third eye activation

Heart's transfiguration

Now wisdom's your own

Within hear the chanting

With new understanding

False constructs disbanding

One with sacred Om

171

Awakening

The merging of the Soul with the sacred energies.

The activation of Chi and the raising of Kundilini.

Merging with the Holy Spirit.

Different cultural expressions.

One truth.

The road to enlightenment,

The merging of heaven with earth.

172

Choose truth. Live it. Make it your own. It is your choice, but it is His gift.

173

It is our own judgement, evaluation and comparison which tells us when we have had a good day or a bad day. The only reality in the 3D world is the reality which we give it, the only meaning, the meaning we give it. It is an illusion based upon our standards of comparison and the standards of the world illusion.

Think about it.

174

Children – Ambassadors of Love

Remember the children when you need inspiration. Remember their boundless joy and the wonder which they freely share. Remember the feeling in your heart when you watched them at play, and you will remember the pathway to Heaven. Their purity and unconditional love literally hold the gates of heaven open so that the divine energies from above might flow to earth and remind those of us, de-sensitized by the world illusion, of our true home. While the world tries to make us forget, our children help us remember, and in the remembering we become light bearers for others. Remember their gift for they will need to draw upon it, when they travel through adolescence and the teen years. In time they will have children of their own and the cycle will begin anew.

175

Thank you for another day to love.

Thank you for the song you put into my heart.

Thank you for the family and friends you have given me to share with.

Thank you for loving me.

176

The Path Under Our Feet

The path to the father finds its way under our feet the moment we love. We don't really find the path, rather it finds us as we love another. Once it has found us, we can't help but find our way for every step will be upon the path. We only lose the path when we set aside our love. Then, although we may be standing on the same spot as when we were last on the path, the path has moved away from us. Love and it immediately returns to its home under our feet. Our earthly direction is not of importance. As long as we love, we are on the path.

The path is not an earthly path. It is a heavenly path. Once on it, its shadow on earth becomes brighter and each step on earth holy and beautiful. The earthly step is a reflection of the heavenly step, the true step upon the path. Love and you are on the path to heaven. All earthly steps will take care of themselves. The earthly steps are the effect. The heavenly steps are the cause.

177

Song for a Teenager

You say we don't love you, but know that we do

We don't get along , but you know that's not true.

You say that you try, but you can't seem to please.

That you're in our lives, we give thanks on our knees.

The angels they brought you, a pearl of great price.

A gift full of promise, a precious new life.

We held you so close, praying never to part.

Your journey in this life, now ready to start.

You're growing, and stretching your wings, set to fly.

Sometimes you fall down but are stronger each try.

We give you our love to help strengthen each day.

As parents, our light's there to help show the way.

Robert H. Wellington

So follow you heart, it won't lead you astray

Your mind is its servant, together they play.

The journey commences, adventure awaits.

Your loving intent is the key to all gates.

Our quest is to launch you, not stand in your way.

Our joy leaps within, as you follow Love's Ray

Our hearts are connected, through loving we soar.

These truths they reside within your very core.

We're all on this journey, many paths to one end.

The answers revealed as you round every bend.

And many are cheering, who have traveled before,

You are never alone as you pass thorough each door.

178

It is the pouring out of our Love that fills us.

179

Emptiness does not come from not being loved.

It is the result of not loving.

180

A Meditation Experience

Pondering the nature of creativity my mind suddenly flashes the idea that, 'The creative process can only be a gift from the heavenly realms, a gift of expression through thought, movement, language and light.' A grateful awareness overtakes me and I enter further into the present moment. Time slows, yet my Soul is quickened. My heart leaps with gratitude, such a reward is the present moment. I slip deeper into the silence of all potential, yet I am aware of all around me. Awakening only takes place in the present moment. Perhaps they are one and the same. The future and past have no meaning here. Only the present exists.

181

The Trail Home

Alone in my thoughts that long to be shared

The fragment of light that shines through the tear

To put into words all that's revealed

The lofty and fine so often concealed

Our hearts hold the secrets, sent from above

The key to unlocking them, always is Love

Their language is silent peaceful bliss

Known only through prayerful experience

The first step is taken as we start to give

To all those in need in this life that we live

Although it's a choice we must all make alone

We journey as one on the trail to our home

182

There is no life without Love, only empty existence. If we walk away from Love, we walk into emptiness.

183

Liniment for Our Soul

Love is liniment for our soul. Love leads to the quiet place within where joy resides, a place without future or past, only present. Pure peace, love, and deep gratitude reside here. It is a place of revelation. Some call it the present moment. Others call it heaven. It is both. It is Spirit's gift to us, heaven on earth. Out ticket to enter is Love given freely and without regard for return. Love given freely and constantly in the present moment, without worry of past or future is pure communion with God.

184

Fatherhood

The blessing and challenge, the joy of giving,

The creativity and energy required to let your inspiration shine on your growing child with just the right balance of Love and firmness.

The constant vigilance to let your heart be your guide, impossible to manifest on earth without much prayer and heavenly assistance.

Find your inner point of light through which the Father in heaven shines upon us all, through which the children see love,

Through which we all return home.

Motherhood and fatherhood stand together,

Guideposts for the children to find their bearings,

Around which the family revolves and draws strength.

185

Another Day

Another day of thankfulness, another day of giving

Another day of hopefulness, another day of living

Another day to spread his love through actions, thought and song

Another day to stride towards Him, our home where we belong

We walk the land with joyous hearts, we see Him in all nature

From smallest insect on the ground to every living creature

Beyond the seen to all that is, beyond uncharted space

His joy and love it teaches us, so we can feel his grace

We reach out with our hands held high, so we might sing His song

Sweet melody it lifts our hearts, we've known it all along

This is the journey, this our quest to bring His Love to earth

To love and give, establish truth, His kingdom given birth.

186

A Thought from The Prophet

"Sing and dance together and be joyous, but let each one of you be alone, Even as the strings of a lute are alone though they quiver with the same music."

- *Kahlil Gibron's* <u>The Prophet</u>

His music is what binds us. Knowing and becoming one with the vibration manifests as love on earth. We must bring beauty, goodness and truth into the world, "by quivering with the same music." Each must vibrate in his or her special way adding to the blended perfection of His symphony.

187

Vibration

Be loving and all around you will resonate with the same vibration. Be the tuning fork around which others with ears to hear will resonate. Vibrate with love, joy and compassion. God's laws will take care of the rest. Let your light shine and the world will be touched by your beauty. In this way we give effortlessly. Such a gift is forever and will never fade. It is a beautiful thing.

188

Particle or Wave, Food For Thought

Science has theorized that all things from the smallest manifestation to the largest structure have both a particle and a wave aspect. The smaller the item, like photon or atom, the more active its wave expression. The larger the item the more active its particle expression. Nevertheless, all things seem to have both aspects expressing themselves to various degrees.

Relating this to the spiritual world, one might say that our everyday earthly existence in our bodies is particle like, separate and individualistic. Whereas a more enlightened expression is more wave like, one with all. Perhaps enlightenment is the realization of our wavelike nature. When we are expressing our particle nature it is hard to see past our separateness, but when we become wavelike the truth of oneness becomes obvious. Was Christ expressing His wave like nature when he walked on water or through locked doors. Were holy ones who have translocated or levitated also expressing their wave nature. Is the process of merging with our true self a process of merging with our wave expression? This is where science and philosophy merge, where the manifested world and spirituality reveal their common ancestry.

Think about it.

189

Meditation Transformations

Quietly, subtly, deep within we slowly change as we meditate. As we hold our mind in perfect peace, our internal wiring changes and habits and desires are replaced by grace and calm knowing.

190

Anger

Anger, where does it come from? Why is it so hard to control? Why do we feel like we have been violated once it subsides and we are ourselves again? Of all the emotions, anger is the one that feels the most like some overwhelming energy from outside has taken over, doing its damage and then receding to some unknown cave deep within. In its place only shame, guilt, sorrow and a strong desire to somehow blame another for this loss of control. It is always the same. Never does one feel better after expressing anger.

One part of yourself says, "It was not me. It was anger precipitating this darkness." The heart responds, "Yes, it was anger, yet I am responsible and must right the wrongs my altered ego participated in."

How well we know that anger is not us. How difficult to sometimes control. Often with anger we are not angry until later after reviewing the incident over and over in our minds. Realizing this, it becomes clear that anger is self-generated, brought on by judgement and related reaction. Without judgement anger fails to appear. It has its roots in judgement, and if judgement is the cause, then forgiveness is the cure. Judgement is at the root of much misery and must be healed before anger dissolves into the illusion that was its genesis.

191

Happiness is a choice. Choose happiness and the world will never disappoint you.

192

Time and Timelessness

Try to imagine consciousness with no time. Remove time from the equation and we begin to glimpse the infinite. Add time and we return to the finite. Time and space are of the world. The infinite is not encumbered by either time or space. Time has no form and yet it is a critical component of all creation. Time is necessary in our 3D world, but the essence which gives all life is from the One. The essence behind life is not of time and space, but of timelessness and the infinite for which there are no adequate words. Living in the present is the first step in merging back with the essence, the first step in transcending time and space, the first step on the pathway home.

When time stands still there is no time. There is no space. There is only the blissful all. Touch beauty and time stands still. Time is a biproduct of where our consciousness is focused. It is not the determining factor of consciousness. On earth, we live in time. In heaven we live in timeless bliss. As consciousness rises, time slows, until we touch the All where time does not exist.

When we raise our conscious awareness, we raise our resonate vibration. They say that at the speed of light, time stops. Has a transcended consciousness touched the speed of light?

Food for thought.

193

Time and Light

God called for light and time began.

From nothingness the dust was formed

Combined with moisture life arose

The light of creation, both particle and wave

The doorway between earth and heaven

The doorway to the Holy Grail

The relationship between light and time

Are they aspects of the same essence

Can one exist without the other

In contemplation, time becomes timeless

We touch heavenly realms and take on a deeper light

This light is different from the light of creation

This light resides in timelessness

It is our light and thus we, in true essence, are also timeless

194

Revelation Never Stops

Revelation never stops for those that seek. Sometimes it reveals itself in leaps, sometimes in small steps, but always it comes, onward, ever onward. The journey is one of purifying the mists which cloud our consciousness. Love is our constant companion.

195

The Essence Behind the Form

We are not just these wonderful bodies. We are the essence which quickens matter and gives it life. Over the eons we have come to identify with the body, limiting the unlimited which is our true self. If we step back and view our bodies as a marvelous instrument, a tool through which to experience His creation, then we will begin to recognize that we are the essence behind the form.

196

Become the Silence

Go within the silence, become the silence, and know you are the silence. We cannot go to the silence and await the mystery to unfold before us. We must become the silence, for there within is the revelation, there within is the mystery.

197

Gentle Presence Deep Within

Gentle Presence deep within,

Walking in my footsteps, carrying me over deep chasms,

Setting me down in the midst of fragrant flowers.

With you all is possible. Without you I am nothing.

Your power flows through me, if I but let it.

You are all that is beautiful, good and true.

All that is in me is you, if I so choose.

All that I am proud of is you.

All good acts are your love running over the edges of the cup of life you have given me.

All good choices and decisions are merely you reflecting out through me into the world.

I am nothing without you.

For how can a beam of light be separated from its source, a wave from the ocean?

198

It is the noise in the mind which hides our true nature. It is the silence that lets it blossom.

199

We stand at the threshold of the birth of our remembrance. The key to crossing the threshold is to know we are already there.

200

Identifying with the process puts us in the middle of the illusion. Identifying with the cause puts us above it.

201

Silence the mind and we silence the noise of the world. Silence the noise of the world and find Heaven on earth.

202

I Love, Therefore I Am

When one is truly living life, love is their guide. **Lead with the heart. The mind is the servant of the heart.** When you sincerely say to someone, "I love you." Is it you who loves or is it God within who loves? If the Father is love, then our loving is a reflection of the Father. If the Father and Love are the same, when we say we love someone, aren't we reaffirming our oneness with God. Think about it.

203

Nourishment for Body and Soul

Pine scent, quaking aspen leaves, the wind rustling the forest canopy

Birds singing, the touch of the breeze on my skin

The sound of a mountain stream, the majesty of endless mountain peaks

The beauty of sculpted cliffs, the silence of the wilderness

Sunset's crimson colors painted across the horizon

An elk feeding stealthily in the meadow below

The scurrying of small creatures going about their business

Reflections off a mountain lake, waves gently lapping its shores

Clouds drifting across the sky

Tiny flowers along my path looking up at me

Vast expanses of grass undulating in the wind like ocean waves

The forest shares its beauty with me and I send my joy back to it

I vibrate with its heartbeat

Truly this is a garden for the Soul and nourishment for the senses

204

Just Words

A Holy One, if in the listener's best interest, can spell out in great detail the steps to enlightenment. But those searching will only know the way by resonating with the spirit within. Until then the words of even a Holy One are just words.

205

Always There

Always there, it sings its song. We hear it in the distance at first, but as we turn towards its vibratory perfection something inside begins to dance . In peace we are lifted to the heights of its inspirational expression and find ourselves becoming one with it. Not by a new revelation do we become one with it, but by remembering.

206

The pathway home is illuminated by our Love and the glow of the footsteps left behind by those who went before.

207

Between

Between all thoughts

Between all words

Between all actions

Lies the holy realm of perfect peace

Here the noise of the world cannot enter

Here rests the cradle and the throne

Of beauty, goodness, truth and joy

The reflection of which heals the world

As it creates new perfection of conscious intent

Quiet the mind and know this place

For it is your true home

208

Thoughts To Ponder

Deep we travel, trying to find the I within. That which is the All behind the All. That which inspires the eyes to see, the ears to hear, the mind to reflect, the feel of a touch, and the aroma of a Lilly. Here resides the One that observes all it creates, watching, learning, playing and blessing. Here the One in the silence calls us with the allure of perfect infinite potential. Here we hear the song and like a magnet are pulled toward it. We are drawn to it because of its transcending beauty, but we are also drawn to it because of its familiarity. Just like the sacred hologram which at the time of creation, perhaps the big bang, spread its infinite shattered pieces, each with the mystery of God imprinted indelibly within its being, throughout the cosmos. Each a peace of God, and thus all evolution which followed is also of God. We are of him. His very essence comprises each of us. Therefore, there is no separation. We are of Him and He comprises us. We are one with him and with All. So who is calling and who is listening. If Source comprises all, then isn't the one calling, also the one listening.

209

Thoughts That Stretch

Are the joy of searching, the joy of discovery, the joy of action and the joy of being, merely different folds within the same cosmic tapestry? Are we threads within the tapestry longing to find, understand and embrace the whole? Could the tapestry be God's cosmic playground, a playground where all of us play many parts? Do we find oneness by touching and knowing each thread and in so doing discover the secret of the whole?

210

Humility

Our humility is an invitation to the Lord to take His rightful place on the thrown within each of us.

211

Kindness

Kindness, such a natural state, yet so often forgotten in the bustle of everyday activities and pressures. Kindness is always appreciated, but generally unexpected in today's world. This is wrong! Kindness should be as natural as breathing is to life. Let your kindness show and it will grow, becoming an ever increasing part of you, until it flowers into full bloom and you become the embodiment of kindness in your every thought, action and word. Others will respond to your kindness and the seed of kindness within them will germinate and grow like the morning light of sunrise spreading across the land. Soon only it will be your expression, and previous false expressions will be no more.

212

People of goodwill spread their compassion by moving their ego aside and getting out of the way. Then compassion flows wherever needed like air into a vacuum.

213

We only know Love when we give Love. When we give Love, we are truly alive.

214

Who Are We?
A Dialog

The answer to this one question answers all questions. This question haunts all seekers on the path. Ponder the dialog below and perhaps we will find the answer together.

Who am I? Am I this body complete with its thoughts, feelings, emotions and desires? Am I my thoughts and feelings? These things seem connected to my body, brain and nervous system. Yet when my body is no more, these things too will cease to exist. Why do I refer to my body as 'my'? Who is the 'my' behind the body and what will it be when my body is no more? Am I energy? Yet isn't energy an aspect of creation and manifestation. It seems there must be something behind the energy, an aspect which is the purpose behind creation. Are we spirit? If so, what is spirit? Is it the silence found in deep contemplation? Is it pure Love or is Love the highest and purest form of energy, emanating from purpose. Is Spirit, purpose and cause, or is Spirit behind purpose. Is Spirit pure intelligence and knowing? And what is pure intelligence and knowing?

To answer the question of who we are is to answer the question of what is God? It seems that God can only be known by something beyond the human form, and the fact that these questions are being entertained is strong evidence that something higher than the manifested body is searching for an awakened understanding of Spirit. I submit, it is Spirit longing to know itself, and thus that which is the essence of our manifested state is the Spirit behind all. Thus we are of Spirit. We are truly His children. By choosing Him, we begin to understand.

215

More Thoughts On Who I Am

Who are we when we breath our last breath and the light of thought is no more? Is there only silence? Are we aware of the silence or have we ceased to be?

I close my eyes and know that I am something beyond my thoughts, something beyond touch and feeling but I wonder what? My human mind cannot connect with it, yet I know it is there. I do not know it in my thoughts, yet somehow I know it in my heart, and my heart wants desperately to share it with my mind and any who might listen. It is unmanifest and yet my body knows it, somehow recognizing that it is a reflection of something true and real. My mind searches in vain for words to describe the light which my heart has revealed, but no words exist to describe this mystery except through metaphor. In some higher sense am I it? Is it me? What of my thoughts and body? What role do they have in this cosmic play? Am I here to learn to know myself, to know the Father, to recognize my relationship to Him, or to learn that we are not and never have been separate from Him?

But why the mystery? Why not just reveal these things? Theologians have postulated that we are given free choice and must choose Him to know Him. Did we know Him before creation or did He need to divide through the process of creation, and manifest through us so that He may know Himself more completely? Many scriptures seem to indicate that heaven's greatest joy is when we recognize our Oneness with the Father. Is recognizing our Oneness with the Father the same as the Father recognizing His oneness with Himself? This process of differentiation of the One through creation, followed by at-one-ment, or a reuniting of the One, may be how the infinite becomes more infinite, a process which the logical mind cannot grasp but perhaps faith can accept.

Just some thoughts.

216

The Kingdom

See yourself as a part of the whole

Be joyful for others successes for they are your own

As are their failures

See the joy in others and know it to be your own

See their sadness and know it also

This is the compassion of Oneness

We are not separate

We move together in an intimate dance

Those who isolate themselves are truly lonely

Those who embrace the whole, discover the kingdom

217

Dare to claim your oneness with Heaven

The choice is not to join His perfection

The choice is to recognize that you are already there.

218

His Gift to Us is Us

The universe is God made manifest. We are a part of the universe and a part, without limit, of Him. His gift to us, is us, and all. He is not separate from His gift, nor His gift from Him. Without the Father all would cease to be, for He is All. How can we be separate, except through our own misguided choice? We have been gifted a choice, a choice to know and be a part of the truth. And in so choosing, God knows himself more completely, as we are His witness.

219

Pierce the Veil

I look at you and know my joy and in my joy I know myself. Joy and Spirit are inseparable and when I feel joy I know it is you dancing with me and within me. Your joy becomes my joy. My joy becomes yours. But how can this be unless we are not really two, but one. And if we are joy, are we not also Love? The intensity of this revelation pierces the veil of separateness. We stretch our wings and begin to soar. This is His promise, a promise already kept.

220

Fatted Calf and a Ring

Love is the path and instantaneously upon stepping upon the path we are home. The Father greets us with a fatted calf and a ring for our finger. We have awakened from a long dream that was full of learning to differentiate between the real and the unreal. It was a dream worth dreaming, but now we are awake and leave it far behind to dissolve into nothingness.

221

Nature touches us most deeply when we know we are the ones doing the touching.

222

The belief that we are separate keeps the Spirit within a prisoner. Know your oneness and release the prisoner.

223

If we choose to take the first step, Spirit will carry us the rest of the way.

224

A noisy mind is the great separator. Quiet the mind and the illusion of separateness dissolves into the nothingness from which it came.

225

Climb the Mountain

Hold tightly to the warmth in your heart.

Let it grow and express itself with each thought and act of kindness.

Be patient with others for they too are climbing life's mountain.

Feel the compassion which comes with the realization that all are struggling to let the Father shine through.

We are all in this together.

Their successes and failures are yours.

Just as your successes and failures are theirs.

Know this and serve unselfishly,

For such an act approaches the divine.

226

Beyond

Beyond all religion, beyond all belief systems rests the truth. It doesn't matter which belief background you come from or currently practice, eventually the search for God will lead you beyond them to pure understanding. There you will find your loving self, staring back at you. This is why the quest is compatible with all great religions and loving belief systems, each serving as stepping stones along the path home, the path to peaceful transcending truth.

227

Above the Winds, Beyond the Sea

Truth is out there, waiting for me
Above the winds, beyond the sea
Yet within grasp, without a step
The deep within, it represents
The purity of a kind thought
He welcomes me, yet all I brought
Was nakedness and Love for all
The purity before the fall
All else I left behind on earth
They served me well in my great search
But were not needed in the end
The answers weren't around the bend
But right inside, the golden fleece
With tears awaited for release
Compassion opened up the lock
And onto earth the Shepard's flock
Spread love and joy, forgiving song
Their beauty hidden for so long
And now His kingdom sings on high
We once had crawled, but now we fly
Through Him we know His sacrifice
Illusion revealed by endless light
For what it is, illusion lies
But now we see with opened eye
And so his Love becomes our own
The harvest in, from seeds long sewn
And we no longer separate are
No longer will confusion mar
The truth for we are now at home
And never were we all alone

228

The Silence Behind The Plan

In the silent place within resides the perfect one, forgotten by many but never gone, patiently waiting for the day of renewed discovery.

In the silence dwells unlimited potential and unlimited possibilities.

It is here that we awaken, find ourselves and begin to live.

A loving life manifests the silence without, from the ever flowing spring of beauty within.

Within the silence, Spirit's plan unfolds and we and all creation are the beneficiaries.

229

Contemplative Beingness

When fortune smiles and you find yourself in pure silence, remain quiet and open your heart, for you are being refreshed and transformed. All around you may be chaos, but in silence you are removed from all distraction. Surrounded by Love, transformation must progress. Remove yourself from all thoughts and know. These thoughts may be from you, but they are not you. Watch them float by. Without the energy of attention, they will soon disappear leaving no trace. In the silence, only the observer, which is you, Spirit, and unlimited potential reside. You are not separate from it. It is the womb from which we all were born. It is that to which all will one day return. It is the essence of which we are an unlimited part. Merge with the essence and establish God's kingdom on earth.

230

And Yet It is Everything

Be your love, let your light shine, for in reality that is all you are, and yet it is everything. Your love carries you through life and then lifts you beyond, when your Soul journeys on. It is that which is permanent, your treasure on earth, as it will be in heaven.

231

See and Identify

See the Lord in all things and identify with all that you see. Let His Will become yours so that your every move, your every thought and word, is His, and yet you cannot distinguish yourself from All, nor All from yourself. This is a life well-lived, a life lived more abundantly.

232

God bless this day and God bless you Father, for you are the day and the night and all that is.

233

Blessing All

I cannot bless my family, friends, or those in need without blessing you for you are my family, friends and those in need. I cannot bless the winds, the rains, the earth and all that exists without blessing you for you are the rains, the earth and all that exists.

So this day I bless you for in doing so, I am blessing All.

234

Ageless Beauty, Fragrant Flowers

Ageless beauty, fragrant flowers
Loving glances, cleansing showers
Time without end, or beginning
Perfect peace, that heals the sinning
Purifying, light from heaven
Shares with us, the bread unleavened
Holy Love, on gentle breezes
Warming us, when all else freezes
Gratitude, leaps from within
When the children's prayers begin
Lead us Lord, to gentle waters
Guide the young ones, sons and daughters
Lift up all in life who fear
Comfort those, who hide their tears
Help me lord to do the same
Sight to blind men, strength to lame
Serving you, the Love inside
Dissolve ego, dissolve pride
Reaching out to all that's true
Greeting all like morning dew
Serving All from Love's great tower
Ageless beauty, fragrant flowers

235

More-I Am

I am the wisp of wind that touches my face
I am the songbirds symphony
I am fresh water bubbling from a spring
Connected by love, I belong

I am the inspiring aroma of every living flower
I am the firmness of a mountain range
I am the devotion of a family pet
Connected by love I am never alone

I am the freshness in the mountain air
I am the unselfishness in a loving act
I am the refreshment in an alpine lake
Connected by Love, I attract peace

What is the I Am which makes me one with all
So patiently it waits, struggling to be known
Everything it is, Father of creation
Connected by love, we are the light in all

236

Flickering

Flickering, His morning light dances on my closed eyelids. He welcomes me to a new day and I am filed with joy. Refreshed I begin a new daily cycle. What a privilege He has blessed me with.

237

Aloneness Becomes Oneness

He is love, yet we are love. He is goodness, yet we are goodness. In a very real sense, as we realize Him, we realize who we are. As we realize who we are, we see through the great illusion of separateness, and our aloneness becomes oneness. In the silence all is clear and for the first time we begin to truly live.

238

The Holy Spirit

It comes like a wave from beyond perception and rolls over and through one's entire body. Intense vibratory energy combined with a feeling of weightlessness, uncontrollable shaking and the intensity of flowing electricity. Re-establishing its sacred network through every nerve and nadi, it pulsates as a powerful wind, overwhelming all other sounds. It is like an overpowering electrical massage, tangible but indescribable.

It is called by some a visitation of the Holy Spirit, by others, Kundilini, chi or psychic energy. Mystics of all spiritual practices are familiar with it. It is the energy behind awakening, healing, levitation, bi-location, ESP, and on and on. Most importantly, it is the energy behind life and creation itself. It is the Spirit within each one of us, released through prayer and meditation to merge with the One Spirit, the Source behind all. It is an expansion experience, following the natural progression of spiritual evolution, the blending of form and spirit, the journey of the prodigal son.

239

Nature's Dance

Rustling trees, summer breeze

Calling us to recognize

In the dance, take a chance

Live on earth but touch the skies

Feel the ground, hear the sound

Sacred drumbeats from within

Find the bright inner light

Once you see then you begin

Feel the toil, work the soil

Smallest efforts find reward

Loving feet, keep the beat

To the truth you journey toward

Joyful time, life sublime

Dare to live a life complete

240

Reach Inside

Activate your love. Let it glow through you. Share it through your smile, a kind word, a loving thought. Lead with it. Make it a part of everything you do or say. Let it guide. Do not look for someone to intercede on your love's behalf. The gift is yours to give. The power is within you.

Embrace true love and it will lift you to your natural state. When we are consumed by love we reside in the present, where there is no room for worry. Hope turns into reality and faith is actualized into a pure abundant loving life for you and all you touch. You will appreciate beauty in all things because you have become beauty. Your relationship to All has become clear for you are a part of All. There is no separation, only seamless oneness and unique individuality existing as one.

This is the great mystery which someday all will understand. Our uniqueness is part of the great whole. The great whole blends each unique strand of the tapestry into one cohesive ever expanding whole. Upon realization we can never be the same. We have returned home, but we have not left our uniqueness behind. Rather we have bridged the chasm of illusion separating the physical from the Spiritual, connecting the two worlds so that they become one. When the gap is bridged, the heavenly chorus is deafening, for this has been our quest since the beginning of time, to merge the higher with the lower. "Thy kingdom come thy will be done, on earth as it is in heaven," has become a recognized reality. Love is the bridge. It is the vibration which binds all together. It is the path which leads to itself, which leads to home.

241

Patience

Loving patience deep within

Silent service now begin

Penetrating healing eyes

Open hearts now energized

Inside bursting from your chest

Gifts from God, love never rests

Tirelessly sending forth

Love and light, pure gentle force

Serving others, know the truth

One with All, as He's with you

Mysteries reveal His song

We have all been lost so long

Never separate, you are one

With His Love the true born Son

Loving patience deep within

Heavenly truth, has always been

242

Subtle Yet Eternal

Reach down, let the essence of who you are flow from you. It is so subtle, yet so eternal. It is your love. It is your goodness. It is you. This essence, this love, this truth is of the highest vibrational frequency, healing the chaos of the world which too many consider normal. But chaos is not normal. It is the natural result of putting our minds first, ahead of our hearts. Listen to the song of your heart. Let your mind serve that sweet melody and watch your lives blossom.

243

The Portal of Love

Expand through the portal of love to an unlimited world. Loving service is the way, the cause and the effect. Here abundance is carried on the wind to all. Here joy permeates all that is seen and unseen. This joy is pure Spirit. The acts of service are pure Spirit. The fulfillment we feel, when contemplating beauty, is pure Spirit dancing with itself through us. Our forms are matter and consciousness swept up in the arms of Spirit expressing its perfection. This organization of matter, quickened by the Fathers word, results in consciousness on the material plane as it is on all other planes of existence. With each step home consciousness becomes less restrained until we reach the purity of His perfect consciousness and expression, unrestricted in any way from the density of matter in the 3d world. This is not to say that matter is devoid of Spirit, for He created matter with his word. It is just to note that consciousness becomes more crystalized in denser realities. Thus matter is Spirit, since God's word, differentiated and guided by Spirit comprises our bodies, our souls, and all that we are. Our quest is to fight through the levels of consciousness by raising our vibration to subtler levels where we resonate more completely with His. This is what Christ and many of the great spiritual masters were able to do. We call it transfiguration. I believe that this was his gift to us. "I am the way," He said. In this way He is leading us to the truth, which He as an elder brother had already discovered. Transfiguration is a process which all of us will experience as we follow Love to His sacred feet.

Love, unselfish giving, forgiving, gratitude, joy and virtuous living are guideposts along the road to awakening, the road to enlightenment. They are not transfiguration in and of themselves, but they lead us to it. Transfiguration is so far beyond our consciousness to comprehend that we will only understand its truth through its process, and the ultimate beingness to which it leads.

The Father has presented before us a quest so wonderful, so exciting and complete that words cannot describe, even through analogy and metaphor. What more fulfilling way to live our lives than to passionately pursue this great adventure. It is the very reason for life itself. It is the construction of the bridge between the higher and the lower. It is the process of creation at its highest level completing itself. Our passion sweeps us into his heart, and then we finally remember.

Until then we must constantly check our spiritual compass as we pursue the journey home. There is no better way to live. All other pursuits waste our precious earthly time.

244

Give It To The Wind

Fill your heart with love and then give it to the wind. The wind knows where to direct it. It does not need a target. It is never wasted. As it dances throughout creation it grows and simultaneous with its healing in the universal it fills you with its endless flow. You cannot give without receiving.

245

Love Is

It is the vastness of space

It is the thundering quiet

It is the endless expansion and contraction

It is concentrated peacefulness

It is the knowing and the becoming

It is the beginning and the end

It is the destination and the way

It is the young and the old

It is us and we are it

It has always been so

Love and know

246

Compassion

Compassion is nothing more and nothing less than the recognition of Spirit in all and all in Spirit, the recognition of Oneness.

Compassion is an energy, shining from within upon our awakening.

Compassion is giving.

Compassion knows that Love can never be divided.

Compassion longs to reestablish this truth.

Like a mother, it fights for its children, and in so doing fights for itself.

247

Deep Within

Deep within it sings its song, calling, ever calling. What is this essence deep within that struggles to be known, but will not show itself without invitation? So humble, so pure, so fragile yet so indestructible, and powerful beyond description. Always singing. Always perfect. Patiently present. With a tear He waits for us, knowing that He is the creator of all, and only His essence can heal the world from its misguided choices.

Listen for Him. Invite Him in to you inner table. Wash His sacred feet with your tears. Embrace the truth shining from His eyes. Be healed and rise to your destiny.

248

Fear versus Love

What is fear but the absence of Love. What is the feeling of loneliness, separateness, depression, failure, rejection, and danger? They are all bi-products of the absence of Love. Love is of the Present. Fear resides in the past and future. Fear resides where Love is not. Love like electricity must flow. Give unceasingly of your love and you will find yourself in the present, where fear cannot enter and Truth resides.

249

True Understanding Transcends

True understanding transcends the mind. The mind has knowledge of the manifested world, gained through earthly experience, but the wisdom of Spirit is gained only through Spirit. Quiet the mind and find the peace within. In the silence all will be revealed.

250

We do not bring Love into our world by inviting it and then waiting for it to come. We bring Love into our world by Loving.

251

The Permanent and the Eternal

Love is the Source of all, the permanent and the eternal. Loving brings us into rhythm with our true Source. Love and become one with His sacred flow. Do not fight it. Move in harmony with it. Fighting the flow is unnatural and can only lead to pain and sadness. For we are a part of Him and thus a part of the flow. How does one move against himself or herself. Love is our choice, but in the end, the only choice.

252

Claim Your Heritage

Claim your heritage. It is the only way. Our heritage is loving Oneness. Some refuse this and wander aimlessly through life, disconnected, lost and unhappy; wondering, "Why Me?" They have rejected who they really are, and thus reject harmony. They must turn from this confusion. A loving thought or word is the internal switch which instantly heals and restores the harmony which is everyone's birthright. It is the connection that allows Him to flow through us and into the world. Just as a flame brings light to a dark place instantly, so a loving act, word or thought instantly dissolves the illusion of being separate, from each other and from God. Find this truth and bring it into the world. It is our quest. It has always been so.

253

The Ultimate Adventure

Love and embark on a journey that was planned for you at the dawn of time. It is the ultimate adventure and the ultimate reward. It is a journey into the unlimited, a journey of service and a journey of boundless joy. It is an adventure in pursuit of the Holy Grail. Upon discovering the unlimited, we discover ourself looking back at us. We discover that we never really left.

254

Companions on the Quest

In your true quest, let gratitude, generosity, patience, understanding and a readiness to forgive be your companions. Let compassion be your gift and observe as the treasure of love fills your coffers.

255

Ask for love and you will receive little. Give love and watch your cup fill and overflow. Giving is the spring which always flows and never dries.

256

The Struggle

Looking within, struggling to know the truth.

Sending love, compassion and comfort out into a seemingly cold world.

Feeling the pain of the displaced and longing to see them held in God's embrace.

Knowing that your pain will never subside until their thirst has been quenched, dedicating yourself to service.

Trying, failing, and trying again to put compassion out into the world.

Small acts of kindness adding up to larger acts.

Seeing Love as the only answer, the only savior, the only way.

Knowing our connection to all.

An act of kindness to one, is an act of kindness benefiting all.

Each act of kindness a step toward the Father.

Each step soon multiplying geometrically.

This is the way.

It is the only way.

257

All Who Would See

I see the small wildflowers blooming
Endless fields of yellow, red and blue
Within their glory He resides for all who would see

I see the wind blowing the tall grasses
In perfect patterns they wave in the breeze
Within their glory He resides for all who would see

I see the morning mists rising from still lake waters
Morning brightness shining through the fog
Within their glory He resides for all who would see

I see greatness in a child's face
With wide innocent eyes they come to teach
Within their glory He resides for all who would see

This is the glory of His gift
This is His very presence
Through Love we see His glory
And share with all who would See

258

Magnetic Fields – Love Fields

Just as a rotating magnet creates electricity and conversely, the flow of electricity creates a magnetic field, so the flow of Love creates a field of spiritual energy around each of us. The more Love we share, the more the flow, and the more intense the field of spiritual energy around the senders and receivers. This is our shield against darkness. This is our gift to the world. This is the vibrational light which dissolves all illusion and reveals the true man.

259

Feel His Presence

Close your eyes and feel Him tangibly within. With each beat of your heart, know His presence. He is within you. He is your very essence, your very life. He is all life. He is all. Realize this and let beauty become your very essence. It was always beautiful, only now you can see it more clearly, and what joy such a realization gifts to the awakened. Through faith we move toward enlightenment. Through Love we manifest it on earth. Throughout the process, Joy is our companion. Joy is pure energy created through the process of recognition. Without limit, it flows to us and from us. Others will feel it in your presence and will either choose to recoil from it temporarily or identify with it, and in so doing create more joy. Ultimately, all are inspired by it. In their search others find the source of joy within. In sharing, the process grows and is continued.

260

And So It Begins

And so it begins.
Without direction by man it starts.
We have only to find the quiet.
We have only to know His peace.
And then standing at the portal of joy, we choose Him.
Upon choosing we are swept up by His loving flow.
We recognize something about this bathing energy,
A kinship, a subtle comfort.
Releasing our fear to the light, we surrender.
At first just a small step,
Like putting a toe into the water to check its temperature.
We find the water so inviting that soon we are immersed.
Moving with its loving currents we recognize it as ourself.
Separation has given way to total union.
The mysteries of the universe are revealed to us.
We see Him everywhere and in everything, and He in us.
Joy is our constant companion.
Giving and receiving freely, we do His work.
Effortlessly we share His bounty.
We have come full circle and found ourselves waiting at the beginning.

261

Know This

Know that God moves through us as He comprises all that we are.

Know that we are never separate from Him, nor He us.

Know that there is no place for evil within us unless we make room for it by choosing to push God out.

Know that even then, evil is an illusion that we created.

Know that choosing God frees us of all illusion.

Know that a loving heart can never be separate from God, for love and God are One.

Know these things and never be alone, for aloneness too is only an illusion.

Know that you are loved beyond your greatest imagination.

Know that you are Love.

262

Esoteric Awareness

An attitude of givingness opens your subtle senses, intuition and esoteric perception onto the world. It is as if the vibrations of a giving consciousness are the very waves that intuitive awareness travel upon. Just as what we can sense through the visible spectrum of light is limited by the size of the photon, and for very small objects the electron; so, subtle activities are detected by loving waves or the higher vibrations of beauty and goodness. Are these higher vibrations also tied to extrasensory perceptions or ESP? *Worth pondering.*

263

The Call and the Reward

Animated by the song of Spirit, life flourishes on our fertile planet.

Purifying rains sweep the sky of dust and refresh the earth in perfect balance with its needs.

The Mockingbird's song alerts my ears to the arrival of morning.

The pulsating heartbeat of life matches the beat of my own heart in perfect synchronicity, and I am at peace.

Something transcending the senses is at work here, something magical and mysterious, but so familiar to the heart.

I am overcome by the sweet nectar of Joy, the gift of union, His promise and our birthright.

The truth behind life begins to reveal itself to me, but I cannot put it into words.

It is like a flash of insight, an innocence, a loving understanding, a great humility and a feeling of unlimited freedom and gratitude.

It is all these things and so much more.

Love is our guide to this place of absolute peace.

Love is this peace, the pathway and the goal,

The call and the reward.

264

A Father's Promise to His Children

Despite what challenges life presents. Despite what may come, I am here for you. Shining in the darkness, all my light is yours. Crossing the abyss together we will succeed. We will together serve Him with all our strength. I see Him in you and it is that which is cherished. You are that. There is no separation. 'I am that,' and we together are one, never apart. My strength is His as it is yours, and yours is ours. Only the mind is confused by the illusion of separation. The heart is not fooled. Let your heart lead. We serve Him and the greater good, not ourselves, yet our needs are more than fulfilled when we do His work. Follow your heart and it will lead you on a glorious quest, a quest we shall achieve together. I am always here for you. It has always been so. Take my hand and we will soar, for we are love and nothing can withstand our Joy.

265

Fatherhood

Love, strength, protection, wisdom, kindness, sacrifice, forgiveness, unselfishness, steadfastness, gentleness, understanding, courage, nurturing – These are the qualities of Fatherhood, that we as fathers must strive to keep foremost in our consciousness.

From piggy-back rides and Mr. Fix It, to counselor and protector, these are characteristics manifested from a father's Love.

There is only one perfect Father and we must let Him be our guide and example. Love is fatherhood. Be your love and become what all children need. Radiate perfect Love into the world, uniting it, healing it, and inspiring the children and all those receptive, to do the same. It is that easy. It is that hard.

God bless the children

May Love be their way

May Joy be their reward

Thank you for Fatherhood

266

You Have Only To Take The First Step

A loving life is the ultimate quest. There is no greater adventure. There is no pursuit more rewarding. The ultimate excitement is a life well lived. All else is empty. Do you have the strength and courage for such a quest. The thrill of the journey is beyond comprehension. The road is paved in light and love and truth. It is narrow to some, but easily traversed by loving steps. Love and it is clearly revealed. Fail to love and you will not even be aware of its existence. Traveling the road of Love is the beginning and the end of the quest, the objective and the reward, a journey into unlimited realization. You have only to take the first step.

267

Rebirth

As I ponder your great beauty, I begin to know you.

Resting in your Joy I am joyful.

As I observe your smile on children's faces, I begin to smile.

Feeling your Love for all that you have made, I love all.

In your silence, I become the silence.

Within your majesty of nature, I am the wind and the rain, your gentleness and your power.

I dig in the earth and touch you.

I swim in a cool lake and you touch me.

I breath and you are inside of me.

I pray and I am inside of you.

I look at a morning dew drop and see your perfection.

I look at the stars and begin to know your majesty.

I embrace my family and know your Love.

I feel your Love and am rejuvenated.

I love and I am reborn

268

Never Separate

Never are we separate from Spirit. Only the human mind struggles with awakening from its separate dream. Love knows not of it. Lead with your Love. Only when the mind is the servant and balanced partner of Love will you know peace. In peace you will know His majesty and know it to be home. Follow your Love, complete the circle and know the beginning anew. Then Joy will accompany all your steps, and separatism shall have faded back into nothingness. This is how it should be. This is how it always has been.

269

All It's Reflections

True Love and all its reflections, including - beauty, goodness, truth, justice, joy, and freedom, is the cause and the result of unifying oneness. It is a unified state of mind. Yet it is so much more than a state of mind. It is realized reality, truth and clarity. Follow truth and experience revealed enlightenment, the true causal state behind all. Beyond our senses you will find it. Armed with clear sight you will see it behind all creation. It is vaster than all the greatest minds that have ever lived can comprehend. Only by uniting with the One Mind will you begin to know.

270

Find yourself in the Silence where only the infinite resides. If you encounter anything other than Love, you are not in the Silence.

271

Like an optical illusion, the truth resides in plain view, and yet remains hidden from us.

272

Between the Thoughts

Searching for the listener
Searching for the one between thoughts
In the quiet He resides
In the realm of the unlimited He is
Patiently He waits
Waiting for recognition
Waiting to be rediscovered
He is the motivator
He is the cause
He is the true reality
He is all possibilities
He is all that exists
He is the quiet
Gently He calls all life
Passionately He sings His song,
Which booms in the silence
Irresistibly we dance to its melody
In perfect harmony we join in His song
Soon we realize that we too are the singer
We too are the song
The symphony in our heart beats with the one cosmic rhythm
We are not different from it
We are it and it is us
We dance on the path where only a few have tread
Yet there are enough to save the world
God bless those that hear
Blessed are those that search

273

A Soft Breeze

A soft breeze disturbs Nature's rest
Sunlight finds its way to the forest floor
Song birds serenade from the canopy above
Silence gives way to the hum of life

God's energy quickens me, causing me to smile
I watch as the observer
I participate as God's hand
I am both watcher and participant

I marvel at its mystery, as Spirit smiles at my wonderment
Is it experiencing It's infinite nature through me
As I discover my oneness through it
It is omnipotent, and yet finds Joy
In observing It's infinite nature with me

And so manifestation arises in its many aspects
Rediscovering its one true nature
Rediscovering its one true origin
It is the dance and the dancer, the cause and effect

The breeze blows again stirring me from these thoughts
This time I know it as a part of me
It caresses me with a lover's touch
It recognizes our oneness with each other
I am content

274

Cross into the stillness fully awake and you will merge with the Father.

275

Diffusion of Consciousness

It is the diffusion of consciousness which holds us in bondage. Diffused consciousness is lost consciousness. It is the sleep of the un-awakened. It promotes a false reality, illusionary and lacks clarity. Coalesce consciousness and the truth reveals itself. Let Love be your implement.

276

Concentration of Our Collective Essence

Love draws us together like a great magnet concentrating our collective essence which, when strong enough, opens the door to heaven on earth. The path thus traveled glows with the light of unconditional love, a glow so bright that others will feel its peace and soon follow.

277

Subtle Pathways

Subtle pathways constantly present themselves to us. They are always there but so easy to miss. Too many of us walk through life half asleep and like a pinball bounce from point to point without realizing our purpose or true nature. Competition and survival consume our days. Life seems to be one reaction after another, always reacting never acting. Actions initiated and guided by wisdom are rarely seen or experienced. He is always sending His love, however, and on those rare occasions, when we are able to silence the noise of the world, we hear Him. At that moment a few are awakened and life begins anew in bliss, never to be the same again. We are constantly given the opportunity to awaken. We have only to claim it. It is His gift. It is our heritage.

278

All This and More

A smile, a friendly greeting, sunshine, a flower in bloom, a bird singing, a kind act, putting others first, understanding, patience, forgiveness, uplifting joy, peace, reaching out to others, recognition of our place in the cosmos, recognition of our oneness with all, the warmth of the sun, letting one's light shine, lending a helping hand, the joy of giving, the joy of receiving, embracing God in your heart, seeing God in all, seeing yourself in all, merging, awakening, embracing, compassion, gentleness, sharing, pure intimacy, joy, sacrifice, wisdom, knowingness, goodness, truth, children, friends, family and justice.

The list is endless. Their message, Love.

279

It does not matter where, who or what we are. It only matters that we love Him with all our heart and all our soul. In so doing, all else will fall into place.

280

Kindness is compassion revealed. Love is compassion in action. Through your kindness, God blesses the world.

281

Somehow His infinite creation was incomplete without someone to share it with, someone with the free will to choose Him. We all are that someone.

282

The Present Revisited

The present moment is lived in the world, but known in the heart.

The present is not outside of you but within.

It is experienced through your passion, while known in the quiet.

The present moment actualizes the past within the potential of the future, all focused in the here and now.

Love guides us to it and stabilizes us within it,

For Love, the present moment and our true self exist as one.

283

Kindness

Kindness, the very breath of the Father; how do we take it from concept to total embrace? How do we become kindness, our true state, hidden by the illusion of separateness and its partner, fear.

Hidden from view, true kindness requires perspective. It requires the rising above earthly constraints to a viewpoint unencumbered by the mists surrounding earthly consciousness. It is a subtle thing, difficult to achieve and more difficult to hold. It cannot be reached by mental endeavor. One must "let it be," and quiet all that obstructs it from view. Then the veil will dissolve and it will reveal its place in your heart, a place it never left.

284

Oneness with the Creator

- John: "… I am in My Father, and you are in Me, and I am in you."

- Bhagavad Gita: "He who sees me in everything and everything in me; shall never lose hold of me."

- Parable: A man is knocking at God's door and when the One inside asks who it is, the man's answer is continuously met with, "I don't know you." The man goes out in the world and begins to learn who he really is. Finally, after eons he returns and knocks on the door. The One inside asks, "Who are you?" The man answers, "It is you." To this reply the door immediately opens.

All of these examples are trying desperately to help us learn who we really are. God is all there is, was or ever shall be. He made all there is with His essence. We are made of His essence. Know this, so when asked at the gate, "Who are you?" you will be able to answer, "It is you."

285

That Which Leads Beyond

The intellect can help guide us through the world of opposites, comparisons, relativity, space and time; but it cannot lead us past this world. Only the heart, higher mind, faith and intuition can lead us beyond.

286

Love Comes In Many Forms

Love comes in many forms, shapes and sizes, The artist gives his or her love through their art, the poet through his or her writing; The true friend through his or her kindness, generosity, patience, compassion, willingness to forgive and understanding.

287

Know Love To Choose It

Love is a choice, but we must know love in order to choose it. Said another way; To love we must take loving action, and to take proper action we must find the love within. This is somewhat of a paradox, a paradox which can only be answered if we start with the premise that Love is our natural state, a state which is always within. But how does one find it within, before having chosen it? The answer is, the mind cannot find it, but the heart can. The heart is Love. Follow the narrow road of the heart and you will know Love. Knowing Love makes the choice second nature.

288

Humility is the emptying which makes room for His Spirit to fill us. All transformative goodness has its genesis in humility.

289

Many learned ones live by the ancient saying, "Think before you speak." The truly wise live by the saying, "Love before you speak."

290

Problems

Problems are crystallizations of thoughts within the mind. A problem is not a problem until the mind identifies it as such, until the mind attaches to it. To clear a problem from our mind, we must first detach from the crystalized thought behind the problem. Clearing a problem is the daily challenge we deal with in the manifested world. It is the opportunity before us; the process of which cleanses the mind of the crystallization and in its place leaves insight.

The Flower Within

Fragrant flower deep within

Softly singing in the night

Ready for life to begin

Blooming forth with golden light

When we open up our heart

Giving with no thought of take

Deeper growth begins to start

All the earth begins to shake

Subtle guidance takes our hand

Firm of step on path so fine

In the presence of the Lamb

Purpose firm in Love sublime

292

Creation

Creating All through just His dream,
A thought so perfect, so supreme.
Pure consciousness soon fills the dark,
All becomes light with just His spark.
Comprised of Love, which must attract,
Small forms begin to interact.
In time these forms transform to worlds,
With suns emerging from the swirl.
Soon life is birthed from Light and Love,
Sustained by essence from above.
Expressing perfectly His teaching,
All known within, yet always reaching,
To become aware of Him,
Within His gift, His constant hymn.
Connecting All through Love and Light,
Till darkness fades and all is bright.
Creation is the journey home,
Of consciousness, once all alone.
A journey, never really done,
Until we wake and have become,
The very breath that started All,
Becoming that which is the call.

293

Seeing All Within Oneself

The wise man knows he's part of all
The very essence of His call
With conscious knowing he observes
With wonder at His sacred word

We're in the very air we breath
We're in the rocks and in the leaves
And they are within us as well
From tiny wave to largest swell

In everything we play a part
And all in us, from very start
The sacred ripples from His breath
Gives all things life, from birth to death

Sacred music, sacred strings
He strums creating everything
Commanding light to fill the dark
The stars and heavens from one spark

With irresistible command
As ocean waves turn rock to sand
His infinite and perfect plan
Created all. Created man

Who as reflection of above
Who's sacred gift is perfect Love
Vibrations which hold all in place
Reflections of His holy face

294

The Sure Road

Make your road Love.

Make it the very fabric of your existence.

Move through, around and within it.

It connects you to your Self and to All.

Let it transmute any false sense of reality, and guide you past the curtain which veils the vast man from view.

Let it restore your soul and put you in touch with truth.

Realization of truth fills the empty heart.

295

A Prisoner by Choice

Deep within the greatest of mountains, He resides. He is a prisoner of the false king of this world, the king of darkness. His power is unlimited, yet he remains a prisoner. We search for Him, but without His light we too are surrounded by the dark. We search for sparks and glimmers of His light, running here and there longing for something lost long ago, so long it is hard to remember just what we lost; knowing only that there is a deep emptiness inside. Why, oh why, wont He free Himself. He is omnipotent. The rocks and earth cannot hold Him and yet, he remains. Why does He not take His rightful place on the throne of light? He just waits. So patiently he waits for those outside the mountain to wake, to remember and to choose. We cry out to the heavens, "Please, what do we need to choose?" And in the silence a small voice whispers in our head, "To choose Him."

Look within and find the light. Follow it and discover your true Self, the Soul which is forever His. Take His Hand and together soar to the infinite. You have freed each other, both bathed in Love. The healing is complete, the world saved. And so it is.

296

The Crystal Cave

The glorious crystal cave lit by the endless flow of His light, with its infinite loving chambers, is only revealed when the shadow of the ego has departed. The ego departs as God is invited in. The silent presence of the essence behind all and within all regains its throne. The choice has been made. We remember who we are and are again whole. The journey has returned to the beginning. The pilgrim is renewed. All is again One.

297

Pondering the Mystery of Sleep

Have you ever wondered why you sleep? Few seem to wonder about this mystery we call sleep. We take it for granted. It has always been a part of our life experience. Perhaps it is evolutionary; a trait that started at the dawn of creation. Surely it was influenced by the rotating planetary bodies and stars. Day and night and the daily experience of light and dark would certainly have influenced the phenomenon we call sleep. But sleep seems more than a habit developed over evolutionary eons. It seems to be a need, not only on the physical level, but on many levels. I have met few individuals who didn't relish sleep. Certainly sleep restores the body, but does it also restore consciousness? Where are we when we sleep? Where is our soul?

Do we exist on multiple levels, multiple realms, which are equally or perhaps more important than our focus within the physical realm? Is our existence a fractal of unlimited dream experiences and time lines that we participate in during sleep, during dreams. Is a part of our consciousness always in these other realms? Is physical consciousness only available in the physical realm, and thus our primary focus of awareness at this time? Will we retain this focus until we learn all that it has to offer, and then transition to another realm, within the endless crystal fractal, as we journey home to the Father? Are we learning and experiencing on multiple levels simultaneously? They say the great ones are fully conscious when in the dream state. Is this the objective of the physical experience; to reunite a fractured consciousness divided between sleep and awake, and reconnect the physical to the higher realms? This deserves deep contemplative analysis, for it is clearly hidden. It is rarely mentioned in conversation, writings or books. My mind and heart wonder why? Think about it.

298

The Breath

What a marvelous thing the breath is.

The rhythmic in-breath,

Followed closely by the outbreath.

The rising and falling of the chest,

Coordinated with the beating of the heart.

Each replenishing the life force.

Neither asking for anything in return.

I wonder at its secrets.

Is there more to the breath than absorbing a cocktail of inert gasses?

Or does the breath give life to the form so that it too might experience life?

Is the body the breaths vehicle for expression in the world?

Is each breath conscious?

Does each use the other in a symbiotic expression of consciousness,

Or is there a greater cause behind it all?

What a marvelous thing the breath is.

299

The Rhythm of Life

Heartbeats, brain waves, the rhythm of the breath, in fact all atomic and energetic vibrations are reflections of the rhythm of life. All that is, responds to this rhythm, this inner drum beat which brought all into manifestation. Beyond our earthly experience the drum beats; think of the stars, planets, galaxies, and the universe, perhaps even the universes beyond. Even the life, death and rebirth of His creation responds to this rhythm, the rhythm of the God, Goddess, All that is. Whatever name you give it, it is the cause of all causes, the heartbeat and breath of all there is, and all there ever will be, all the infinite and unquantifiable; the One behind the All.

300

Compassion and Selfless Giving

True Love resides on a sacred level that we can only touch through aspiration and striving. By aspiration I mean a deep and pure longing for the Father within. This manifests in one's life as Love which guides and points the way. Striving is unselfish service to others. This manifests itself as a genuine caring and compassion for all, with no expectation for one's own gain, although giving can never be made in a vacuum. It always results in the giver receiving countless more than he or she gave. Unselfish service or sacrifice manifested by a deep, pure and sincere compassion causes or enables us to emerge onto the level where true Love resides. It pierces the veil which has hidden it from our view. We come to realize that we are not visitors here. It is our rightful home, a home the long eons had erased from our memory. We cannot will ourselves to this high plateau. We must emerge through the gateway of compassion and selfless giving.

301

Seeing You

I see you in a child's smile

The power of the river wild

I see you in the birds that sing

And also in the wind chimes ring

I see you walking in the woods

And always where there's light and good

You touch me through a fragrant flower

And cool me through a summer shower

I see you in the children's joy

Delighted with a favorite toy

I hear you in the rustling leaves

And so much more when one believes

I know you through a tender heart

The rainbows arch, a swallows dart

I see you in the mighty elk

But also in sweet mothers milk

You are the peace, the gentle dove

For you are joy, compassion, Love

302

Remove That Which Obscures Your View

Like the sculptor who clearly sees the object which he wishes to carve in a piece of marble, and creates by removing all which obscures his view, until only that which was trapped in the stone has been freed; so we must remove all that obscures our view of the final truth within.

303

I am the love I know within. I seek the quiet place within, where the Love that is the essence of All resides.

304

Love is the bridge. Find love, give love and watch it grow. With infinite power Love will encompass all that you are. Love is the door and the destination. Soon there is no need for the bridge, for God has established himself on earth, through the one who loves.

305

The War Between Heart and Ego

The battle between the heart and ego rages. The heart, if chosen, will always prevail, but too often the tongue will cause chaos by insisting on making its position known. Listen to the heart. Learn how to interpret its guidance. It will never lead you astray.

306

Love and you will find your way. It cannot be otherwise. When we truly love, God is within us expressing his perfection. Knowing this is a tremendous joy. He is joy and knowing him can never be less.

307

A successful life is a loving life. Live harmoniously within Love's flow and you eventually become it. We choose by setting aside our will and becoming one with His.

308

Natural Beingness

The man was youthful, happy strong

Love of life, his daily song

Through his love he gained respect

Without knowing his effect

By his actions naturally

He gave to you, he gave to me

He wasn't this, he wasn't that

Expressing love his only act

All could see the light shine through

But he just was, like morning dew

309

The path is an awakening of a part of ourselves which has always been, waiting only to be aroused from slumber.

310

You Are Already There

Living in the presence of God is the realization that you are already there. We have emerged from the essence of God, a part of Him as He is a part of us. His love has given us our individuality and freedom of choice, but we will always be of the one whole. These gifts were given to us so that we might experience revelation through the journey toward Oneness. It is a wonderful mystery, and yet no mystery at all. The mystery dissolves in the light of truth. It is our choice.

311

Joy, The Recognition of Oneness

What is joy but the recognition of oneness, which lights up our mind, when we connect to the greater. Joy is the natural flow of energy which transpires when we touch the greater consciousness and for a moment connect with it. The realization which flows is infinite and remains with us as we try to unravel its omnipotence. It is a download of truth which might take eons to unravel, but is always with us from the moment of recognition to the end of time. We experience this when we look into the eyes of a newborn, when we enjoy the laughter of children playing, when we watch the Fall leaves swirl in the wind, or enjoy the scent of spring flowers in the air. All these things connect us to the Father and give us joy.

312

Love's Magnetism Attracts Love

If you want to be loved, you must love. Love with all your heart, soul and being, and you will be covered up in Love. Negative thoughts repel love. Love exists in the infinite realm of Love. Love, and step into this realm. It is that easy and it is that hard.

313

A New Sense

We are taught from birth to observe the world through our senses.

Thus, when we awaken to something greater than our world we have difficulty holding on to it.

A new sense is required to know the greater whole.

Ironically, it is not a new sense at all. It is not even a sense.

It is our true essence which resides forever in the silence.

It is Love.

When we love we are in touch with the greater whole, for Love is the greater whole.

It is the cause and the result of all that is.

Through Love All is revealed.

314

The Touch of the True Self

Words cannot describe the touch of the True Self. When we love with a tension so concentrated, still and pure, we leap from our earthly temple on wings to the Father. Our physical being quickens as we leave the lower earthly vibrations behind. When we return to our earthly home we resonate with a pureness of knowing a truth we cannot put into words, but is ours forever, as it has always been.

315

Genius

The home of genius lies deep within each of us. Focus and one-pointedness is the key to unlocking its secrets. Genius is not a random event. It is an ability to touch the realm of knowable things. This ability has been given to each of us. Some have learned how to use it. Most are unaware that it is a gift given to all, thinking it is merely a random genetic anomaly. Yet most of us have had unexpected moments of brilliance. A still mind is required. Meditation can lead us closer.

316

Pick Us Up

Gentle, flowing,

The essence of that which is at our very core

That which is us, that which "I Am"

Love, compassion, sacrifice

These are our true qualities

Each reflecting the true essence of our being

All else, a great illusion

I Am Love, which is all

Lord, let us live this truth without faltering

But if we fall, pick us up that we might try again

And with each effort, take another step closer to you

317

Constant State of Thankfulness

Love is living in a constant state of thankfulness. The future holds many secrets but we can only find our true direction by discovering and following the love within.

Kahlil Gibron in his classic, <u>The Prophet,</u> says it so well, "Do not try to direct Love's path. Love, if it finds you worthy directs your path."

Let Love direct your path. Only when we subordinate our will to His; only when we put ourselves in his hands; only in this way can the journey home be completed.

318

Become the Witness

Being righteous and knowing what is right are often disconnected in daily practice. Choose righteousness. Plant the seed. Nurture the seed with daily meditation, service and spiritual discipline. Let Love and Joy be continuous throughout the day. See all mankind as brothers and sisters, fathers and mothers. Do these things and witness the oneness of all life as it reveals its beauty. This revelation is the rainbow bridge which connects heaven and earth. It is always present, but rarely seen. Let your vital energy transform into light and love; the purified essence of all there is. This essence illuminates the pathway home. As we travel home, we will leave His blessings with all we touch along the way, for we are one with Him, as He flows through us. We have only to choose.

319

Quiet the Mind

One of the greatest gifts we can give to the world and thereby ourselves, is a quiet mind. Quiet the mind and you will find the truth behind all. It has always been there but the turbulence of our thoughts, like the ocean in a storm, hides what is underneath. When the ocean is at rest a beautiful reef teeming with life and color comes into view. Just so, a quiet mind reveals its majesty.

320

Each Day Brings a New Opportunity

See each day as a new beginning, a new unfettered opportunity to come closer to the Spirit which is behind all creation, motivating all. Let the Holy Spirit direct. It will lead you unto His sacred feet, beyond comparisons, relativity and the pairs of opposites, beyond the mind to the One. Many are lost within their thoughts and desires; ever comparing all that they see, do and say with the world.

Our natural tendency is to better ourselves and this is a good thing, but too often this betterment is based upon mental analysis and standards established by the ego and not the heart. Let your heart lead, and loving improvement and growth be your goal. The gifts which will surely follow are from the higher realms and will remain within you throughout eternity.

321

The Earthly Trap

Constantly our mind makes comparisons and both the haves and have-nots want more, based on these comparisons. The mind is a marvelous creation, but it is designed to compare within the world of duality. When the mind is put in charge we fall into the earthly trap of never having enough, never being satisfied. Such a life can never find peace, for peace resides beyond the pairs of opposites, beyond the comparisons, beyond the earthly mind. Peace lies within the heart. Quiet the mind, open the heart and rise above the wants and desires of the mind. Let the Spirit within rise to the surface. Become one with it and it will lift you to a point high above the chaos of the egoic world. Here you can begin God's work, with your feet on earth and head in heaven. Here comparisons melt away in the clear light of Love. Giving of this Love now becomes your way. Taking is seen for what it is and left behind.

322

The Father of Vipers

Fear is the father of the vipers, anger and hate. Together they attack our innate goodness. Aided by their allies, the illusion of separatism and discontent, Fear's only desire is to destroy beauty, wherever found. It often accomplishes this by entering our psyches through the back door. Fomenting righteous indignation, for some perceived inequity. It takes up residence within our psyches, pretending friendship and concern. It plays on our fears and anxieties. We fear we have lost something. Perhaps economic, perhaps a perceived loss of prestige or social status. Whatever it might be we fear we have somehow lost it, in the past, or will, in the future. We feel a deep discontent. We think we are alone in whatever injustice holds our attention. Fear begins to morph into anger and ultimately the illusion of hate. Our emotions take over and any hope of rational thought and forgiveness is lost.

The solution and healing from this false premise, lies in the present moment. Fear of the past, or of the future, cannot reside there. Stand guard at the gateway of thought and refuse entry to anything that is not loving. In this way the illusions of past and future fears are starved of energy, and soon dissolve away. In the present, only the light of truth surrounds your every word, thought, or action. Here is where you can see clearly. Here is the firm foundation from which you can serve.

323

The Bridge Between Worlds

Enlightened Man, the bridge between worlds. Built photon by photon as he roamed the world searching for the forgotten answers. No stone was left unturned as he proceeded. All earthly pleasures tasted. They were sweet to the pallet but sour once consumed. Finally, after eons of searching, and ready to give up all hope, he turned within. Upon turning, the journey began anew. Slowly but with increasing certainty, he cleansed his psyche until the light of his basic goodness was bright enough to light his way. To his wonder, a bridge appeared, a bridge that he himself had constructed as he was remembering his Oneness. He had not seen it before, but as his inner light regained its glow, it was revealed. Each of us is building our own rainbow bridge. Find your inner light and you will soon remember.

324

Devotion

It is not the saint, or holy one that we must be devoted to.

It is the Love within them.

It is the Love within us all.

Follow it. Become it, and live in the light.

325

Beyond All Thoughts

Beyond all thought lies our goodness.

It waits to be discovered so that it might again sit on its throne, the throne within each of us. We cannot will it to rise with our mind. Rather we must quiet the mind so that its light can be discovered.

326

Finding the quiet within and then recognizing it, is challenging and difficult to master. It requires tenacity and perseverance. **But oh the joy of doing so.**

327

A Little More

Each day we must –

Love a little more

Forgive a little more

Be patient a little more

Serve a little more

Express beauty and goodness a little more

And be our true selves a little more

See, know and be through Love

Feel Love and know God

Express virtue and express God

Know that God is behind each word, thought or action

Choose God and be a witness, as God serves God through God

328

Follow Love – Banish Fear

"The kingdom of God has come, only men do not see it."
(The Gospel of Thomas)

Worldly interests and pursuits, veil the truth from us. Evil's presence seems to grow stronger by the day. Drugs, gangs, family disintegration, wars in the name of god, or racial jealousies, fill the news programs and media. If we could just exchange 1-2 selfish thoughts each day for 1-2 thoughts of brotherhood, putting others first and service, we would complete the long climb out of the abyss. We are the 'me' generation, stooped in selfish thoughts of greed and fear.

Fear is the tool of evil. It is the path to Hell. Fear of not having enough, leads to greed. Fear of something different from yourself leads to stagnation and racism. Fear for our own wellbeing causes us to hide our light under a bushel. Fear of being alone causes us to seek other false friends, like drugs and alcohol. Selfishness springs from fear and has contributed to the deterioration of the family and the Love which should reside there.

But fear is an illusion, the child of separative thought. We are not separate. We are One with all, eternal beings of light. There is no death, only the continuing evolution of the soul on its journey home. There is no aloneness, only the illusion. We are all One. We have only to give of ourselves to realize this. Giving is the secret passage beyond the veil. Giving with Love and without expectation of return is the highway home, the highway to His Kingdom. We have only to open our eyes.

329

Your Heart Knows His Beauty

Look for God within. His beauty immeasurable, beyond comparisons, beyond the pairs of opposites. Your heart knows His beauty. He is not separate from us. This is hard to express adequately in words. But it can be known through the heart. Hard to grasp and harder to teach, for earthly vibrations cannot approach the divine. But it is waiting for all who truly seek.

330

Never Alone

We often think we're all alone
That no one cares; why should they?
With eyes downcast or on their phone
We cry as our life slips away

So many exist but do not live
They think they have nobody
Another day to just survive
Just coping, never knowing

Withdrawn from life, afraid to look
Or believe there is an answer
Fears manage us, so much they took
Worse than malignant cancer

But we are not alone my friend
And never were or would be
The darkness only works through fear
Find courage and begin to see

Yet we are just a breath away
From breaking from dark's grip
Pure joy must be our only way
Let God's winds guide our ship

So long, before, the world seems right
Declare a perfect day
And you will find the sun will shine
You've bested, come what may

Sweet energy will flow from thee
And worlds will be renewed
So know the truth, it's light will heal
Before your prayer is through

For all of Life is there to share
You never are alone
Just find the strength to love and dare
And know how far you've grown

And with your choice, hear heaven's cheers
For one of theirs has wakened
Now strong stand firm, your voice is heard
And never can be shaken

Through you now others hear the word
His song through you is sung
And happiness expands within
The healing has begun

And all because you chose to Love
Truth's beauty now unfolds
The World is healed, your friends are saved
Fear runs before the bold

Broadcast the truth through your example
We never are alone
With eyes which see, God heard your plea
All darkness overthrown

331

Healing

Healing is a unifying and strengthening of the energies which flow around and through each of us, vitalizing us and enabling conscious awareness. When we are sick these energies have become disoriented, disconnected, and restricted. By reuniting, reinvigorating and reorganizing these energies the body again becomes a fully functioning whole, and its natural state of health shines through. A healthy body reflects the heavenly harmonics of His word. An unhealthy body, for whatever reason, has restricted this flow, and disease, deterioration and decay fills the void where health once resided. Find your natural balance, through good food fresh air, pure energized water, exercise and sunshine and your natural health will bless your days.

The Smile Within
(To all the Teens)

When things seem darkest
Days seem grey
Dark tries to make your brightness fade
And you feel lost within the haze

Take a deep breath

Just feel your heart and then begin
Look deep inside and find that grin
The magic that has always been
That awesome smile that's you within

When insides churn
With high school blues
You think all eyes are judging you
You plea for deliverance from this zoo

Take a deep breath

Just feel your heart and then begin
Look deep inside and find that grin
The magic that has always been
That awesome smile that's you within

Robert H. Wellington

When close encounters now unfold
When darkness seeks complete control
With people playing many roles
It's time to find more lofty goals

Take a deep breath

Just feel your heart and then begin
Look deep inside and find that grin
The magic that has always been
That awesome smile that's you within

Within us all is a rare gift
To be released when we're adrift
When shared with Love, our hearts will lift
All those who search and seek assist

Take a deep breath

Just feel your heart and then begin
Look deep inside and find that grin
The magic that has always been
That awesome smile that's you within

Look and see your Love transforming
Calming winds and all that's storming
Greeting all with a new morning
A new earth and sky now forming

Take a deep breath

Just feel your heart and then begin
Look deep inside and find that grin
The magic that has always been
That awesome smile that's you within

And so we heal with each encounter
Like a wave spreading to all
Now you're running, once were crawling
Through Love's light we all stand tall
Just remember when you need it
Love is always there within
Make the choice to share its magic
The secret is we all are kin

333

Remembering Love

Remembering Love, to know it's presence and to see it behind all things is often forgotten in the rush of earthly activities. It is always there, but too often requires a painful event to encourage us, to draw upon it, and regenerate ourselves within its glory. Keep your love in the forefront of your consciousness. See the Father in all. From life's successes, both yours and others to the scurrying of the smallest insect, Spirit is in everything. We have only to see Him, and His light will shine through each who sees and bless the earth.

334

Birthrights are claimed not given. Claim your birthright as one with Spirit and come to realize who you really are.

335

Let joy be the road I walk upon and endless compassion be my greeting to the world.

336

Open My Eyes

May I always know that you are smiling with me and we are one, in all I see, hear, smell, taste, touch, think and do. May I always be aware that you are the aroma of the flowers, the sweet singing of the birds, the majesty of the mountains, even the industry of the smallest ant. I pray with all my heart, "Open my eyes."

337

Messiah

They say, in times of need, when a million voices cry out to heaven, His Light and Love become more intensely focused on earth. The world calls for Love, and one, great in Spirit, perhaps a prophet or messiah will be born to heal, comfort, uplift and free the world from its bonds. **Such a time is now.**

338

Prepare Yourself

The cries of God's children are reaching to heaven and His Light and Love are descending. Prepare yourself. Open your hearts and minds to accept and receive this light and love. The Lord dwells in those whom he finds worthy. The key to the kingdom is to Love. Love all, love yourself, those good to you and even those who are bad. Love those you know and those you don't, love all. Love the beauty and balance you see in nature. Give, forgive and understand. Unselfish service is the surest way into His kingdom. Most of all, serve without any expectation of return. Loving service is its own reward. Such service puts you squarely in Spirits flow and firmly on the pathway home.

Communion

Communion, pure and gentle, yet all powerful

Our natural state, if we but know it and have faith

Through communion we become one with the One

From the gentleness of a soft, cool breeze

To the power of the universe

It is His glorious gift, offered freely to all,

The quest of the wise

Recognized by the pure of heart

Lived by the meek and humble

Experienced through love

At-one-ment through faith

His greatest wish is that we accept His gift

It is "the Love of the Lord of Love which consumes all selfish desires and sense cravings tormenting the heart." *Bhagavad Gita*

Communion is withheld from no one

"It is the Fathers good pleasure to give you the keys to the kingdom of Heaven." *Bible*

340

Satiated by Spirit

All beauty, all passion, all loveliness, all joy, all that we long for comes from God. There is no desire that cannot be satiated by God's Love.

341

Passion

Beauty is the reflection of Heaven on earth. When we long to behold beauty, we are longing for the Father. At the root of our passions is a desire to reunite with God. When we see passion as separate from Spirit, we lose our bearings, stray down the wrong path, and suffer the consequences of swimming against the heavenly flow. We must not be ashamed of our desires and passions, for these are heavenly gifts, but they must be directed toward God who is all good, beautiful, passionate, righteous, just and free. Our passions, lovingly directed will carry us to the gates of Heaven. Passion misdirected is short-lived, empty, and unsatisfactory. Passion directed toward God is forever, and leads to eternal life.

342

Longing to Know Itself

The longing of Love to know itself, the driving force behind creation might be explained this way.

> Love longs for itself
> God longs to know God, which is Love, which longs for itself
> Man longs to know Love, to become Love, to know God
> And ultimately merge with that so long sought

If we see our passions as a longing for the Father, and direct them accordingly, we will soon find Him. He is the Love which we carry inside. Love is our true essence and guide. Faith in this truth leads us to at-one-ment, enlightenment and abundant life. These concepts become plain to those who truly love, to those who are kind, gentle, forgiving unselfish and compassionate, to those who have become Love.

343

A Prayer

Oh Lord

Thank you for your Love which manifests in so many ways

A Love which is without end

Unveil your Truth to me that I may do your work more completely.

Forgive me my missteps

Help me to forgive the missteps of others

Let me look upon each sunrise as a new exciting adventure

A new opportunity to Love

Give me strength each day to serve tirelessly through your Love

Help me to know with each sunset that I did my best.

Amen

344

To All In Need, I Pray

I pray for those who feel alone

I pray for those who hunger

I pray for those who struggle

I pray for the persecuted

I pray for the misguided

I pray for the lovers

I pray for those who have forgotten how to love

I pray for the meek and humble

I pray for the injured and the sick

I pray for the earth and all of nature

I pray for the families, and for those without families

I pray for all children

I pray for the parents

I pray for all

I pray for you

And I pray for myself

345

Dynamic love

Love is dynamic, never static. It must flow to be. It flows by being given, and received in return, for Love is reflected in Love, and then given again. With each exchange, it grows. It never diminishes if it is shared. It only fades if not shared; if hoarded or kept to oneself. One does not have to worry about receiving love, only giving and sharing, for Love always returns to the sender. It is His law. It is His promise.

346

The Heart

The Heart is the one truth on earth. Listen to your heart and never will you be misled. Love unceasingly, unfailingly, without reservation, without hesitation, without expectation, and without condition. Only the Heart knows the way of the narrow path.

347

Love Begins With Me

Love begins with me

I am primarily responsible for the love in my life

If I initiate Love, Love will flow

Into my life like an endless river

The choice to Love lies with me, as it does with each of us

It must be chosen

348

Responsibility

Each of us is responsible for our own spiritual evolution. We take each step. No one else can take them for us. Through our Love we choose to walk the narrow path. Through our Love we become a part of all, and it becomes a part of us. We are the center and circumference, but only because we are of Him, and He is All. Recognizing this in ourselves allows us to see the truth in all. This recognition is beyond the senses. It comes from our very essence. It resides in our hearts. It is Love.

349

We Are Not Our Thoughts

We are not our thoughts, although if given energy, they can appear to be reality. They may be good or not so good, like happiness or fear, but they are not of the true Self. We can only know the Self or the I Am, by becoming One with it. It is always there waiting to be asked to take its rightful seat at the throne within. But too often our ego and intellect, our moods, desires, appetites and physical feelings, are sitting there instead. This is because the dark illusions of this world fool us into thinking that they are the I Am. When we recognize our error and choose to set these false friends aside, the real I Am can take its rightful seat, and God's kingdom is restored.

350

Attitude

One's attitude through life; one's happiness, joy, understanding, sorrows, and on and on, are choices, choices which can only be controlled once they are recognized for what they are, and the true self has taken charge.

Our false identification with our bodies, our intellect, moods, hopes, fears and emotions, are at the root of our earthly problems. Setting these aside and living within the Self is the cure.

All things of the body, emotions and mind are effects which must be set aside. They are not us, but all too often we cannot make the distinction and are swept away by their cries for recognition.

Centering ourselves in the I Am is the only way to peace.

35¹

Another Day

Another day of recognition of our oneness with all

Another day of Joy

Another day of loving and giving of oneself

Another day of Living

35²

Labor Day

Every day is a day to remember our true labor and to be thankful

Our true labor is revealed to us from the quiet place

Where only His voice is heard

It settles on our very essence, like dew on a garden, and we know

Labor is a gift to all

Even those who sleep

353

From Sorrow to Joy

Through our sorrow we find and eventually become Joy.

"The cup from which we drink is the same cup that was hollowed by knives."

- *Khalil Gibron, <u>The Prophet</u>*

Our compassion and related sorrow propels us into His arms.

Here we find refuge and are restored

Sorrow can be a stepping stone from the intellect to the intuition

From the world of opposites and comparison to oneness and enlightenment

Through Love we turn our sorrow to Joy

354

A Plea To The Light

That which built our bodies by drawing the substance of the mother unto it. That which is a part of the great I Am. That which is eternal, I long to know, and become again in waking consciousness. Deep down I know that it is me and I it, but the illusions of the world often blind me and corrupt the truth. Whatever the barriers, whatever the challenges, let me have the strength and wisdom to find my way home.

355

Meet Negative Thoughts With Love

Meet negative thoughts with Love and repel them utterly. Love will do its work completely, sending the thought back to the sender. In time the sender will see the nature of his or her negativism, and begin the long, but eternally rewarding climb out of darkness. This is the blessing which heals. This is how we save souls.

356

As a Man Thinketh

"As a man thinketh in his heart, so is he." -*Bible*

This is the key to the manifestation of a loving, serving, earthly consciousness. If we consume ourselves with the fulfillment of our desires and passions, our nature and life will reflect this. If these desires are base, our nature will be base. If they are virtuous, our nature will be virtuous. Of course, our true nature is always virtuous, luminous, loving and compassionate, but its expression on earth is influenced by the gift of choice. We manifest virtue by keeping virtuous thoughts foremost in our minds.

Keep in mind that the body is influenced by the mind. At its purest level the mind is a reflection of the one truth. The higher mind is a temple through which God is expressed. If our mind is filled with trash, so will our expression be trash like. If filled with compassion, so our expression will be loving. This is the process of manifesting heaven on earth.

"Thy kingdom come, thy will be done on earth as it is in heaven."
-*Bible*

Let us set about to do His will on earth. Let us clear obstructions within ourselves and become clear conduits of His grace and endless beauty.

357

Heavenly Vocations

We cannot wait for the Father to offer us employment on earth as His assistant. Each of us must make the decision to do His work on earth and then "Just Do It." The moment we share our Love, we have been hired. Our vocation is where ever we spread our Joy and Love. It does not have to be tied to a religion or charitable organization. Our work is to Love where ever and whenever we see a need.

And there is always a need!

358

The Power Within

The power within cannot be seen, only known

Faith enables us to touch it

Love to know it

Joy opens the gates to its kingdom

Love is the bridge over which it is carried unto the world

Kindness and forgiveness are its seeds

Beauty, the fertile soil in which it grows

Transfiguration, its final goal

359

Quantum Musings

Most of us are aware of the particle and wave nature of light. Beyond this, some physicists propose that all things have both a particle and wave nature. Larger bodies have more of their particle nature expressing itself, while smaller bodies can more easily express their wave nature. Taking these theories one step further into the metaphysical realm, one might argue that the process of enlightenment is one of becoming more wave like. Perhaps the term enlightenment is more literal than we were aware.

Perhaps our higher selves are more wavelike and our earthly manifestation more particle like. Perhaps we were all wave like once, and just as the prodigal son descended, so we descended from the bliss of light or wave expression, to the trials of particle expression. Great teachers have taught that to understand the higher mysteries, we must learn to separate our consciousness from our bodies. Could one interpret this to mean that we must become more wavelike and less particle like?

Waves blend perfectly with other waves, and once past each other they continue their journey with their frequency unaffected. Particles cannot do this. Earthly existence is particle like. Spiritual existence is wavelike. Is this why all holy encounters talk about the presence of indescribable light.

One might argue that particle consciousness is individual and separate, while wave consciousness is individual and one. People who have experienced religious awakenings, spiritual experiences or near death experiences talk about light and luminous entities. Are these great ones, who have become, or learned to express their wave nature? Is there a balance between wave and particle expression which is in fact

enlightenment, or nirvana, or awakening. Is science suggesting that their search for answers has brought them full circle, and the quest for knowledge outside of ourselves, points clearly to that which is within? Has science unintentionally confirmed that which holy ones, masters and saints from all spiritual disciplines have known intuitively for millennia? Look to your wave nature and I think you're answer will be a resounding YES.

360

More Quantum Musings
Just For Fun

Sometime, long, long ago a pact was made with the material world. This pact stated that we could enjoy God's manifested playground, but we must abide by its rules, the rules of matter and the rules of time. Now we know that time and space, travel together, and that matter is only energy dancing in and out of existence. We also know that the mere observation of the dance, of these manifested expressions, can impact the dance and how it is perceived, and thus we play a role in the dance or more precisely, we become a part of the dance simply by choosing to observe. Some men of science, and men of Spirit, have postulated that we are the dance, or more precisely, consciousness is the dance. Thus without conscious awareness there would be no creation. Stated this way the conclusion seems self-evident. We are the observer and that which is being observed simultaneously. As Kahlil Gibron puts it, "We are a boundless drop in a boundless ocean." Thus we are more than our bodies, emotions and mind. "We are a part of everything and everything is a part of us." -*Bhagavad Gita*

How interesting that modern physics, quantum theory and western scientific thought have merged with eastern and western philosophy. We have traveled full circle and met ourselves on the road we started the journey on. The roads leading to the exploration of outer phenomenon and inner experience are ultimately the same road.

361

Know Who You Are

Identify your fears and know that they have no place in God's kingdom.

Identify your selfish attitudes and know that they are not you.

Identify your emotions and know that they are your servants and you are not theirs.

Know who you are and be that. You are the very essence of all there is.

The stardust that forms your body was knitted together by you yourself, as a part of the one great truth.

Be that truth. It is up to each of us to choose to actualize our potential.

Some call it freedom of will. In reality it is the discovery of that which has always been, that which will always be. Pierce the veil by being.

Only illusion stands between us and reality.

362

Creativity

It is the creative process or journey that must be pursued

Not the result

In true creativity the result takes care of itself

When we create we find ourselves living, acting and being in the eternal NOW

At this frequency we resonate with all potential and all possibilities

Our mind is quiet, our thoughts perfectly clear and precisely formed

We are in control of them and not the other way around

Creativity is the voice in the silence

Hear the voice within, and know that you are it

363

Creation

Creating All, through just His dream, A thought so perfect, so supreme.

Pure consciousness soon fills the dark, All becomes light with just His spark.

Comprised of Love, which must attract, Small forms begin to interact.

In time these forms transform to worlds, With suns emerging from the swirl.

Soon life is birthed from Light and Love, Sustained by essence from above.

Expressing perfectly His teaching, All known within, yet always reaching,

To become aware of Him, Within His gift, His constant hymn.

Connecting All through Love and Light, Till darkness fades and all is bright.

Creation is the journey home, Of consciousness, once all alone.

A journey, never really done, Until we wake and have become,

The very breath that started All, Becoming that which is the call.

364

Empty Without You

I close my eyes and you are there

I search my heart and you come pouring out

I am empty without you

My mind can think Love, but it cannot know it without you

I am whole when I let you lead

I am a shell without you

I Am, cannot be without you

You are I Am, and I Am you

365

Sharing One's Light

Some are hiding themselves from the light of their dawn.
Hiding their unique beauty, fearing judgement and scorn,
From the sleepers who wander in their world of illusion,
Fearing light that might waken, from their endless confusion.
Hiding their true expression from the light that reveals,
The joy of Love's nature, hiding behind fear's shield.
Status Quo is their safety, never venturing beyond.
Hiding in self-made prisons, never gifting their sound,
To a world that is starving for the beauty they hold.
Leaving gaps in creation, leaving stories untold.
Which can only be filled by their love freely shared.

Receiving through giving, these must always be paired.
And the great revelation, His gift and His promise,
Deep within it has waited, for the conscious to notice.
And the picture's revealed so that all soon may know,
That the truth is a Oneness, connecting all in His flow.
Freely shared through the eons, yet beyond time and space.
So with courage rejoice from the light of His Face.
For your gift heals the world. Fight through all ridicule.
Such a gift is beyond price. Giving , His perfect rule.
Service wrapped in his Love, nothing on earth compares.
For the law of the heavens, starts with Love that is shared.
And receiving will follow, it is the only way.
Embrace truth and awaken, see the night turn to day.

Epilogue:

And so, these few reflections come to an end. I have shared them to remind us all of the magnificent adventure we are on. Nothing else compares. Each of our journey's are unique, but they lead to the same destination, a destination without end, a destination which is nothing less than a new beginning. This is the quest beyond light, the quest for pure consciousness.

See you somewhere on the road ahead.
God Bless

www.ingramcontent.com/pod-product-compliance
Lightning Source LLC
Chambersburg PA
CBHW060351080526
44583CB00012B/265